The Essence of
Effective Communication

The Essence of Management Series

The Essence of Effective Communication

Ron Ludlow
Fergus Panton

Prentice Hall

New York   London   Toronto   Sydney   Tokyo   Singapore

First published 1992 by
Prentice Hall International (UK) Ltd
Campus 400, Maylands Avenue, Hemel Hempstead
Hertfordshire HP2 7EZ
A division of
Simon & Schuster International Group

© Prentice Hall International (UK) Ltd, 1992

Typeset in 10/12 pt Palatino by
Keyset Composition, Colchester
Printed and bound in Great Britain by
T.J. Press (Padstow) Ltd, Padstow, Cornwall.

Library of Congress Cataloging-in-Publication Data

Ludlow, Ron.
The essence of effective communication/Ron Ludlow, Fergus
Panton.
p. cm.
Includes index.
ISBN 0-13-284878-3:
1. Business communication. 2. Communication in management.
I. Panton, Fergus. II. Title.
HF5718.L83 1992
658.4'5—dc20
91–26163
CIP

British Library Cataloguing in Publication Data

Ludlow, Ron
The essence of effective communication.
I. Title II. Panton, Fergus
658.4
ISBN 0-13-284878-3

5 6 7 8 9 / 00 99 98 97 96

Contents

Contents

1

Effective communication

INTRODUCTION

'Organizations would be OK if it wasn't for the people who work in them', complained a frustrated consultant after an unsuccessful presentation of a communications improvement proposal to a board of directors. 'They don't listen, they don't try to understand.' How much his reaction was due to his own inability to communicate effectively or the uselessness of his proposal is unknown, but ask any manager what one of his major problems in any organization is and he will reply 'Communications!'

What is so important about communication that managers and employees get so frustrated and uptight about it? Why do we need effective communication in an organization? At a personal level, why do *you* need to be an effective communicator?

In this book we will be searching for answers to these questions, and also giving some hints on developing your own communication skills. Senior managers tend to spend up to 80 per cent of their time communicating, in one form or another, with other people: upwards, downwards and horizontally within their organizations, and across the boundary into the outside environment with clients, customers, buyers, sellers and branches of government. In fact, about 50 per cent of a manager's time is spent in generating information. So the importance of developing skills in interpersonal communication is obvious. If you are not a good communicator you are not likely to develop into a good manager! Managing relationships with others is a major part of a manager's job in an organization.

Communication in organizations

But what is an organization? Firstly, it consists of a number of people. Secondly, it involves interdependence. If you had 1,000 people, each of whom designed a product, purchased materials, manufactured, sold and distributed the product, you would not have an organization, you would have 1,000 enterprises. People are interdependent when the performance of one individual affects and is affected by the performance of others: for example, when one person designs the product, another purchases materials, and so on. Interdependence calls for co-ordination of activities which ensures that individual tasks will be carried out so that the objectives of the organization will be achieved. And co-ordination requires communication.

With the acceleration of the efficient use of information technology, the nature of managerial relationships is changing. Managers of the future may have fewer subordinates but rely more on information systems. Relationships between colleagues then become more critical to the success of the organization as information needs to be transferred and integrated across internal boundaries. So, as a manager's role in gathering and passing information increases, his skills as an interpersonal communicator will determine his effectiveness.

The context to which this book relates is the organization, and we will be concentrating primarily on people communicating with other people within it. People spend over one third of their adult life at work, and any improved communication skills developed there will spill over to improve the quality of their personal life.

What is communication?

Communication can be considered as a personal process that involves the transfer of information and also involves some behavioural input. Communication is something people do. It does not exist without people taking some form of action. It has all to do with relationships between people. It can be very complex or very simple; very formal or informal – it all depends on the nature of the message to be passed, and on the relationship between the sender and the receiver.

It consists of the transfer of information and understanding between parts and people in an organization, and the various modes and media involved in communication interchanges. Effective communication therefore is critical to the success of an organization.

Look at the changes that are occurring in organizations today:

- They are becoming more complex, both in structure and technology.
- Economic and market conditions are forcing greater efficiency and quality in manufacturing and services.
- Government legislation requires managers to interpret the changing implications for policies and practices in their own organization.
- People at work, especially the younger ones, are expecting more from their employers – not just higher wages, but also greater personal and job satisfaction.
- They are becoming more dependent on horizontal communication channels. With increased complexity, information needs to flow quickly between specialists rather than go up and back down the hierarchy, with its inevitable delays and message distortion.

So when we look at the changes that are taking place in organizations today, it is clear that managers, to be effective, require communication performance at hitherto unheard-of levels of excellence.

Some of the common answers to the question 'why communicate?' are as follows:

- It leads to greater effectiveness.
- It keeps people in the picture.
- It gets people involved with the organization and:
    increases motivation to perform well;
    increases commitment to the organization.
- It makes for better relationships and understanding between:
    boss and subordinate;
    colleagues;
    people within the organization and outside it.
- It helps people to understand the need for change:
    how they should manage it;
    how to reduce resistance to change.

There also needs to be a clear message, which must be understood by the recipient. A supplier might say to a very overdue customer: 'Arthur, I wonder if you'd like to look at your account, it's a bit overdue.' This is rather ambiguous, but if he were to say: 'Mr Jones, your account is very overdue and we are placing the matter in the hands of our solicitors at the end of this week if it is not brought within our normal terms of sale by then', then there would be no doubt in Arthur Jones's mind that his supplier means business!

Managers and communication

One of the classic managerial dilemmas is that of balancing the pressure of short-term results with the need to take a long-term view, as in problem solving and making decisions versus planning, forecasting, etc. Managers have to work within the political reality of their organizations and to recognize that they need to build power bases in order to influence others. This means that they have to (a) develop credibility for their personal and professional expertise and (b) be able to communicate with and influence other managers.

When you consider the nature and purposes of the communication which managers have to carry out, the topic takes on a whole new dimension. The audience might be public or private, requiring adjustments of style. Among the numerous purposes of communication will be the following:

- Seeking or receiving information, allocating blame, encouragement, control, selling proposals, confrontation.

- Talking to different levels within the hierarchy – to individuals, to groups, to departments – and externally to customers, suppliers, banks, other professionals;

- Using both formal communication:
    meetings, reports, proposals, notices;
  and informal communication:
    counselling, advising, talking to other employees.

- Working in different roles: as chairman, project leader, analyst, subordinate, colleague.

- Evaluating communications: are they facts, opinions, gossip?

- Building up networks to obtain real information which may be given freely or concealed – which means you need to ask the right questions, or else you will find yourself drowned in data but starved of information.

- Trying to influence those over whom you have no power.

Managers need to be effective communicators to achieve positive results in today's organizations.

Interpersonal communication

'Communication' is one of those words like 'organization': it is not easy to define. One way of looking at it is as 'an interpersonal process of sending and receiving symbols with meanings attached to them.' It is therefore supposed to result in the exchange of information and shared understanding between people. So a measure of the effective management of interpersonal communication is that information *is* passed, and relationships *are* built.

The success of information passing depends very much on the nature and quality of the information received and this in turn depends on the nature and quality of the relationship between the persons involved. People tend to experience personal satisfaction when communicating and interacting with friends, relatives and others they know well, in fact, with people with whom they feel comfortable. They don't feel the need to be guarded because of the way they manage their relationships with each other. They can speak openly and honestly, and joke about serious matters. Personal abuse is a form of comradeship. But managers frequently have to work with others with whom they have not developed close relationships in order to achieve organizational objectives. Misunderstandings may occur, leading to disagreement and conflict, or often the avoidance of conflict and the development of mistrust. Out of this can develop lack of co-operation and an unhealthy work climate. People are polite to each other, and apparently genuinely co-operative. But because the underlying interpersonal problems have not been faced, the quality of interpersonal communication is poor.

People are different, and we need to understand the nature of those differences and try to modify our interpersonal behaviour to cope with them. You, as an individual, may have a consistent view of the world, your organization and your job, but you have to work in an environment consisting of other people. That is your dilemma. In reality, one of your greatest challenges as a manager is that other people are different from you. Two of the basic differences between people are personality and perception. These differences cause people to behave differently towards others in different situations, and cause communication problems.

Personality and perception

There are nearly as many definitions of personality as there are psychologists! From Freudian sexual repression to Jungian self-actualization to Adler's superiority complex – the list would more than fill this whole book. What we need to know about personality as managers is that we aren't born with it – at least, not totally. For personality is determined and developed by both the influences of our inherited genes and of our social and physical environment and experiences. These give us our unique individual core values, beliefs and needs which shape our consistent behaviour to the world. Once we have reached a level of psychological maturity, our personalities do not change very much, and their components are integrated. What it does mean is that as we all have different experiences in life, and rarely have the same physical and social environment as others, the combination of inherited and environmental factors which interact with each other in complex ways results in patterns of behaviour which are unique to us as individuals. So we vary in intelligence, education, religious beliefs, social background and experiences, and this affects the way we communicate with others.

All these factors create individually different frames of reference, with the result that each person looks at the world in a particular and unique way. Our physical and mental make-up and our environment directly affect our perception and judgment. Perception is the process by which we select, organize and interpret sensory stimuli and information in terms which are consistent with our own frames of reference and view of the world. We are continually receiving information. Some of it we ignore, some we accept and interpret in the light of our past experience to forecast, as accurately as possible, what is going to happen in the future. In this way we form images of people, often based on very little information, predict their behaviour in certain situations, and select what, in our view, is the best way to approach, influence or communicate with them. Too often, when interpreting information, we see or hear what we expect to see or hear, rather than dealing with objective facts. The biggest barrier to objectivity is our self-concept, what we 'know' we are in relation to the world and other people, and we tend to reject information which appears to threaten our self-concept. We just do not want to be told that we have egg on our face, or a ladder in our stocking, and will only accept this information gracefully and without threat from people we are comfortable with.

As we are all different, and our perceptions are different, the process of communicating effectively with other people is rather difficult at times. It is easier when we get to know and understand people: where there is unshared perception, values, and understanding, effective communication is unlikely. How many times at a first meeting have you thought, 'I don't like this fellow, I can't get through to him'? First impressions tend to last, as we tend to reject cues to the contrary when they are threatening to our confidence in 'judging' people.

Figure 1.1 illustrates how to increase objectivity in the way we perceive others, and how to increase self-knowledge. The Johari Window is useful in reducing perceptual bias in interpersonal perception. When we are with other people there are some elements of ourselves, our attitudes, behaviour and personality with which we are familiar and which are also apparent to others (the OPEN area). Similarly, other people may observe facets of ourselves of which we are unaware, e.g. 'he's got bad breath' (the BLIND area). We also tend to keep some of ourselves, our attitudes and feelings, private and do not disclose them to others (the HIDDEN area). And we also know that there are some aspects of ourselves which we do not understand and which are not apparent to others, but which do affect our behaviour – such as suddenly flying into a blind rage for no reason at all (the UNKNOWN area).

When we first meet someone, we tend not to reveal much about

	Known to self	Unknown to self
Known to others	OPEN	BLIND
Unknown to others	HIDDEN	UNKNOWN

Figure 1.1   The Johari Window

ourselves – our open area is small. This often leads to first impressions of us which are wrong. For communication to be effective, we need jointly to work with others to increase the size of the open area, while reducing the blind and hidden areas. This can be achieved by two conscious sets of activities – self-disclosure and feedback. Self-disclosure is giving free information about ourselves to others, so reducing the hidden area, and feedback from others reduces the size of the blind area. When both are used, it can also help to reduce the size of the unknown area, and reveal some of our underlying motives.

EXERCISE 1.1

Objective

To break down self-imposed barriers and receive feedback from others; to identify more accurately your self-image and perceptual biases by sharing information with others.

Process

1. In this exercise you work in a small group (5–7). Each person has a pencil and several sheets of paper; at the top of each sheet each individual writes the name of one of the other members of the group (including him/herself).

2. Each individual then writes on the relevant sheet of paper either:
   (a) 5 personal attributes, or
   (b) 5 work habits/attitudes, or
   (c) 5 strengths/weaknesses

   which he/she perceives in each of the members of the group (including him/herself).

3. The relevant sheets are then distributed to each member of the group.

4. Each member in turn then reads out:
   (a) the perceptions by others of him/herself, and may ask for clarification where necessary;
   (b) his/her perception of him/herself.

5. The group discusses the differences in perception which emerge, and the reasons for these.

Some people may feel wary or threatened by this exercise. It is best to introduce it by explaining the Johari Window, and also initially to concentrate on positive qualities.

This exercise uses both self-disclosure and feedback, and the individual's blind and hidden areas will reduce accordingly.

Time required: about 35 minutes.

To communicate well, we need to know ourselves and our frames of reference and to be able to assess other people. Only then can we hope to find the best ways in which to communicate effectively with them, both to pass information and build relationships. Some of the reasons we do not assess other people well are given below:

- We assume that they are going to behave the same way in every situation.
- We try too hard to put everyone into consistent categories. (Stereotyping)
- We are too influenced by first impressions.
- We are positively influenced where we have common character- istics with other people, e.g. same school, same function.
- We are too influenced by apparent negative points, e.g. if someone is not very good at short-term decision making, we might assume that he/she is not going to be good at long-term planning either.
- We make constant errors because of our own limited frames of reference and self-concept.
- We are not sufficiently interested in, or pay enough attention to, other people.

All of the above can cause us considerable problems in the communica- tion process (see Figure 1.2) which consists of basically four phases:

- sending (via symbols)
- receiving (via symbols)
- understanding (perceived meaning)
- accepting (using feedback)

There is always noise, or barriers to communication, every time the process is conducted. If you are tuning in to an FM radio station, you know that you have to tune in to the right frequency or you will simply hear random noise or a distorted signal. So it is in interpersonal

9

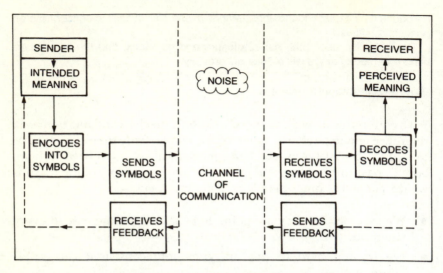

Figure 1.2   The communication process

communication where the barriers consist of such factors as are illustrated in Figure 1.3.

Status effects can occur when one person is considerably higher in the hierarchy than another. The four knights who heard King Henry II say 'Who will rid me of this turbulent priest?' perceived this to be a royal command rather than a statement of anger and despair. Consequently they murdered Archbishop Thomas à Becket, with what they perceived to be Henry's blessing. For this misperception the consequence for them was death, for King Henry II the penance of a barefoot pilgrimage to Canterbury, and for Thomas à Becket canonization.

Semantic problems occur when people use either the same word in different ways, or different words in the same way. Do you know that there are 15 different meanings of the word 'charge' in the English language? They also occur when people use jargon or 'professional shorthand' which they expect others to understand, or language which is outside the other's vocabulary.

Perceptual distortions can be caused by having a poor self-concept or self-understanding, or a poor understanding of others.

Cultural differences affect communication between people from different departments in the organization, e.g. between R&D and production. R&D has a long time horizon, while the production manager is concerned with keeping his assembly line going and

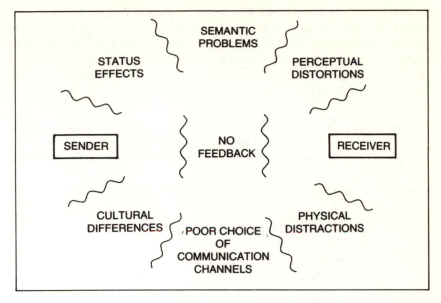

Figure 1.3   Barriers to communication

achieving his daily targets. They also occur frequently between people who have experienced different social and religious environments.

In England an invitation for dinner at 8 pm would see most guests arriving at about 8.15; in Germany punctuality is king; in Greece, 9 to 9.30 might be the norm; in India even later – if at all! In most parts of the world nodding your head means agreement, shaking your head means no – except in some parts of India, where the reverse is true. Communication can be very difficult at times!

Physical distractions cause a lot of noise, often literally: insufficiently insulated rooms with car noises filtering through, poor lighting, a typewriter clattering away in a nearby office; and such things as frequent movement of body posture, fiddling with a pen in the hand, even the arrival of coffee at a critical stage of the communication.

Poor choice of communication channels. If you want immediate action from the receiver, you would not send a lengthy discussion report, you would probably pick up the telephone or go to his office to tell him what to do. Remember also that 'one picture is worth a thousand words', and in this age of computer graphics the information can be produced more quickly in this way too.

No feedback. Although one-way communication is quicker, two-way communication is more accurate. In complex situations it helps both sender and receiver to measure their understanding and it improves their joint commitment to the task. It enables both parties to pick up and correct misunderstandings, leading to a higher quality of reception and acceptance.

Dealing with barriers

Barriers to communication can be classified into three groups:

1. Barriers to reception:

    environmental stimuli

    the receiver's attitudes and values

    the receiver's needs and expectations

2. Barriers to understanding:

    language, semantic problems

    the ability of the receiver to listen and receive, especially messages which threaten his or her self-concept

    the length of the communication

    status effects

3. Barriers to acceptance:

    prejudices

    interpersonal conflicts between sender and receiver

One way of reducing the effects of these barriers is to check continuously during the communication process what the message really is, as illustrated in Figure 1.4. The actions we can take to achieve this are listed below:

Sender

- WHO: To whom should the message go?
- WHY: Why am I communicating? What are my motives?
- WHAT: Decide what to communicate. Be clear about what you need to communicate.

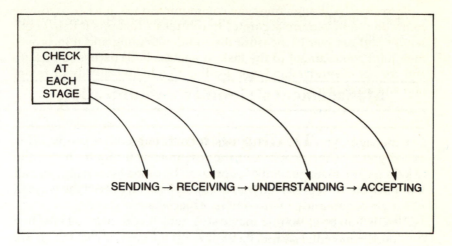

Figure 1.4 Checking communication

- WHEN: Choose the best time for optimum reception.
- HOW: Use language the receiver will understand and which is unambiguous.
- WHERE: Choose a location which will not interfere with the reception, understanding and acceptance of the message: privately? home or away? in a group? at work or outside?
- Keep checking with receiver.

Receiver

- Be fully ATTENTIVE to sender.
- Listen ACTIVELY to the message being sent.
- ASK for clarification, repetition where necessary.
- Keep checking with sender.

Together

- Realize that misunderstandings are bound to occur, and be ALERT for all cues to this effect.
- LISTEN, listen, listen, and listen again.
- TEST your understanding of the message.

- Share OPINIONS, feelings and perceptions generated by the message.

Management style and communication

As a manager, you try to get things done through other people. This means you manage people and the resources you require to get the task done. The management of people can be called leadership, and all of us have our own preferred leadership styles which affect the ways in which we communicate with others, especially our staff.

There is however, no one magic style which will make us effective leaders. We have to work at it, to develop different styles which are most appropriate to the three elements in every leadership situation:

- You, the leader
- Your staff
- The task to be done

Only by understanding and analyzing these three elements can you choose the right style for any given situation. There are four basic leadership styles (see Figure 1.5):

1. Directing
2. Coaching
3. Supporting
4. Delegating

Each of these is appropriate, IN THE RIGHT SITUATION (but we all have our preferred style and often find it difficult to change that style even when we need to).

Directing is most appropriate when a complex task has to be performed and your staff are not experienced or motivated to do it; or when you are under time pressure for completion. You explain what needs to be done, and tell them what to do. In such a situation, you can fall into the trap of over-communicating: excessive explanation can confuse and waste time.

Coaching is appropriate when your people are more motivated and are becoming more experienced in coping with the task. Here you

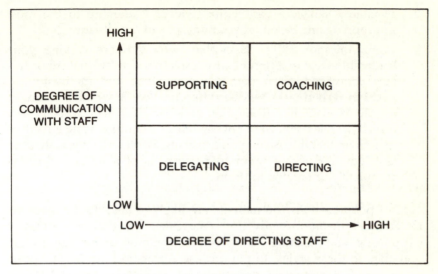

Figure 1.5 Four basic leadership styles

would explain in more detail and help them to understand by spending time building up a good relationship with them.

Supporting works when people are familiar with the techniques required and have further developed their relationship with you. You take time to talk to them, to involve them more in work decisions, to listen to their suggestions for improving performance.

Delegating is right when your staff are thoroughly conversant and efficient in the performance of the task, and you can simply let them get on with it. People of experience do not take kindly to a manager sitting on their shoulders and interfering with every aspect of their work. However, you still need to keep an eye on their performance to ensure that your required standards are maintained.

If you combine the four basic leadership styles with the characteristics and the experience of the people you are managing, you can identify which is the most appropriate style of leadership in a particular situation: you will be using *situational leadership* (see Figure 1.6). To become effective in choosing the right style of leadership – in other words, to change your style to meet the needs of the situation – you need to develop three specific skills:

1. Analytical skills: to assess the degree of experience and motivation your subordinates bring to the achievement of the task.

2. Flexibility skills: to vary your style of leadership to the most appropriate one based on your analysis of the situation.

3. Communication skills: to explain why you are varying your leadership style in different situations to the individual subordinates concerned. Each person's experience and motivation to perform certain tasks will be different. People whom you might usually manage in a delegating style would react adversely to a directing style if you were not capable of communicating effectively to them that the reason you are using a different style is that the task you are asking them to perform is of a nature which is completely unfamiliar to them.

Most people whom you manage are likely to fall into the medium experience, medium motivation categories. So the two styles – supporting, and coaching – will work for you most of the time. But, if you stick to these styles, to paraphrase Abraham Lincoln, 'You can manage 80% of your people effectively for 100% of the time, or 100% of

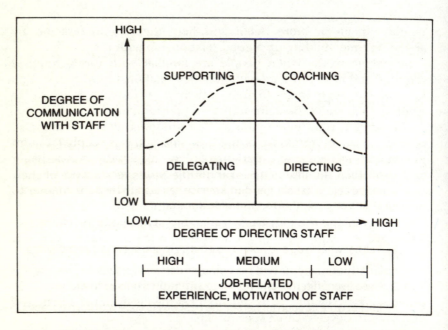

Figure 1.6 Situational leadership (from Hersey and Blanchard (1977) *Management of Organisational Behaviour: Utilising human resources*, 3rd edn, Prentice Hall International)

your people for 80% of the time, but you can't manage 100% of your people effectively for 100% of the time!'

You will need to use all four styles at some time or another, and so you will need to develop the following communication skills:

1. How to explain clearly, and concisely, the nature of the task.
2. How to tell people what to do and how to do it.
3. How to encourage people when work is well done.
4. How to build relationships with your staff.
5. How to share problems with them, and listen to their ideas and feelings.
6. How to delegate effectively, so that there is a clear understanding of what problems people should bring to you.
7. How to explain why you are behaving differently as a leader in a particular situation – why, in effect, you are being consistent in your inconsistency!

EXERCISE 1.2

What is your preferred leadership style?

Consider each of the situations, and choose which action you would normally take:

A. One of your employees has been working enthusiastically and performing her work effectively and achieving targets. You have let her work with little supervision. Recently you have assigned her new tasks which you felt she would be able to handle. Her performance has dropped and she is taking a lot of time off on sick leave. What would you do?

   1. Tell her specifically what to do and monitor her work closely.

   2. Tell her what to do and how to do it but try to find out what her problems are.

   3. Keep supporting her and work through the problems with her.

   4. Let her work through for herself the best way to cope with the new tasks.

B. You have just taken over as a section head. Productivity was moderately good before you were appointed, but it has dropped now, so you want to introduce some changes in work procedures and assignments. Your staff have been unco-operative, muttering about how things were better under their old boss. What would you do?

1. Implement the changes and closely monitor performance.

2. Tell them why you want to make the changes, explain the benefits to them and listen to their concerns.

3. Discuss the proposed changes with them and ask for their suggestions for improved productivity.

4. Leave the group to work out for itself what it needs to do to meet its targets.

If you selected Choice 1 in each case, your preferred management style is likely to be 'Directing'. Choice 2 denotes a 'Coaching' style; Choice 3 a 'Supporting' style, and choice 4 a 'Delegating' style. However, your preferred style may not be the most effective in each case.

In Case A, you have used a 'Delegating' style before giving the new assignments. You need to know what the problems are and help her solve them, while continuing to give her your support, as you feel she can manage the tasks adequately. Choice 3 – a 'Supporting' style – would be more appropriate in this situation.

In Case B, performance was moderately good before you took over. It is likely that your predecessor used a 'Supporting' style. Now performance is dropping and your group is unsettled. Choice 2 – a 'Coaching' style – is appropriate here. However, if the group still fails to meet its targets, you will have to move into a 'Directing' style until performance improves and targets are achieved. Then you can move back into a 'Coaching' style and monitor and control less closely, while building up relationships with your group.

Look at your work situation, and try to identify where you should change your management style to improve your staff's performance – but remember, if you do change, be sure to communicate why you are doing it.

Total communication

One of the major problems in communicating with other people is that it occurs through different channels and at different levels. This is why so many communications become miscommunications. Personal beliefs, values and frames of reference influence the ways in which we send and receive messages. They cause us to communicate through four separate channels:

1. Facts (or what we perceive to be facts, based on our own experiences).
2. Feelings: our reactions on an emotional plane in a specific situation.
3. Values: fairly unchanging beliefs about ourselves, our society and culture.
4. Opinions: attitudes we take about our own position in a given situation; views that are subjective, not objective.

We can use all these channels in any interpersonal communication.

EXAMPLE 1.1

Jim: Liverpool are on top of the First Division again (fact).

Charles: They've been on top most of the season (fact).

Jim: I'm sorry that Kenny Dalglish resigned as manager, though (feeling). They're going to have to beware of Arsenal's challenge now (opinion).

Charles: Well, it is the best football division in Europe (value). Whoever wins it will do well in the European Cup next year (opinion).

Problems arise when you send a message on one channel and it is received on another. 'Jack Nicklaus's record of 17 majors will never be beaten' is an opinion expressed as a fact – but it is only an opinion, although most people would accept it as a fact.

To avoid these miscommunications, we need to understand that messages consist not only of facts but also of feelings, values and opinions of the sender. We need to be able to identify which is which when we decode a message, to make sure we are receiving the correct message. Feedback and active listening can help us to receive and understand the real message. We think so much more quickly than we can talk that often we do not listen to the whole message – instead, we are busy framing our response before the sender has finished. So we really do need to concentrate on listening actively to the total message –

the facts, feelings, values and opinions of the sender. In fact, we tend to use our visual sense to comprehend about 75 per cent of communications – words alone convey only about 20 per cent of the meaning.

Active listening

Active listening requires definite commitment and personal discipline. You prepare yourself deliberately to concentrate and not be influenced by external influences. It is time-consuming and you need to pay attention to the other person on three different levels (see Figure 1.7).

As managers, it is critical to our effectiveness to listen to other people. But we all make conscious decisions on whether to listen, to half-listen, or to ignore communications from them. If the information confirms our current needs and beliefs, and if it helps us to satisfy our current needs, we are likely to listen intently. Information that conflicts with either or both is likely to be rejected – try telling your boss that his department is not running efficiently!

We have to be careful not to discard important information as irrelevant noise. We make choices about listening: you may train a cat to listen to a melody on a piano. Introduce a mouse, and the cat shuts out the melody to concentrate on catching the mouse. People have the same ability. However, the more skilful we are at listening, the better we are likely to be at communicating generally.

Figure 1.7 illustrates how we all communicate through our minds, our emotions and our body language. The mind selects the words which convey the facts of the message. Our emotional commitment is shown in the feelings we express when delivering the message. We use body language to emphasize key facts and feelings.

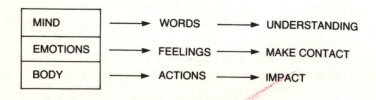

Figure 1.7 Active listening

EXERCISE 1.3 NON-VERBAL COMMUNICATION

1. How do you show:

friendliness	boredom
trust	enthusiasm
fear	impatience
defensiveness	happiness
anxiety	anger
frustration	disappointment
willingness	doubt

2. Can you see when your boss/your partner shows these feelings? Are their gestures the same as yours?

3. What can you learn from this?

Active listeners show their attention, commitment and availability both verbally ('please tell me') and non-verbally (not fidgeting or looking bored). When listening, try not to butt in and superimpose your own views and judgment – the sender has a message for you and nothing is more guaranteed to turn him/her off than jumping in before he/she has been able to express a point fully and clearly. Some techniques you can use to help you listen actively are listed below:

1. Reflecting back
    (a) Content 'What you are saying is . . .'
    (b) Feelings 'You seem very worried about that.'

2. Showing support 'I understand. Please go on.'

3. Checking 'Can I repeat what you said to check my own understanding?'

4. Clarifying 'It seems to me that what you mean is this . . .'

5. Structuring 'Can we look at how this started, try to identify the problem and ways in which we can solve it?'

When to use active listening
A has a problem, B is listening.

1. B knows the solution, A will accept it.   B tell A.
2. B knows, but A wants to be convinced.   B sell to A.

3.   A and B have equal knowledge of the situation.   Discuss together.

4.   A knows more than B about the situation.   B listens and reflects back to A.

Active listening shows you care about not only the communication, but also the sender. It helps to overcome the barriers caused by differences in people.

EXERCISE 1.4 ACTIVE LISTENING

The objective is to develop the skills of listening, reflecting, summarizing, probing and supporting.

Work in groups of three:

A.   Discusses a real personal problem.

B.   Listens and counsels.

C.   Observes, coaches B and gives feedback to both.

Rotate the roles after 20 minutes and repeat.

Things to look for:

A.   Use a real problem, even if it is not important. Do not expect to be given solutions.

B.   Listen for key words, often raised indifferently.
     Use short sentences/silence.
     Guide and control: don't advise, agree or disagree or assume anything.
     Use A's terminology.
     Listen for feelings and needs.

C.   Coach in terms that are practicable and on factors/behaviour that can be changed, e.g.:
     B is using long sentences/words – try using short ones.
     A is not coming clean, B needs to probe more.
     B needs to summarize where you are so that you can move forward.

Organizational communication

Communication in organizations uses two basic channels – formal and informal. Both are important and both carry messages – sometimes reinforcing, sometimes conflicting – throughout the organization.

Formal channels are ones which have been set up by the organization. Messages flow in three directions: downwards, upwards and sideways. The downwards messages consist primarily of information which is necessary for any staff to carry out their work, such as policies and procedures, orders and requests which are passed down to the appropriate level in the hierarchy. Upwards messages are reports, requests, opinions, complaints. Sideways messages are between different departments, functions or people at the same level in the organization.

There tend to be strict rules about the use of these formal channels. For communication to be effective, all three channels need to be open and unblocked at all times. The upward channel is the one which blocks most easily, and when this happens it is an indicator that an organization's policies, procedures and employee relations need to be reviewed.

Informal channels spring up by virtue of common interests between people in organizations – these interests may be caused by work, social or outside relationships. The grapevine is a very powerful channel. It has been estimated that managers receive over half the information they need for planning purposes through the grapevine. Its messages may frequently be distorted, but they often carry more credibility than those coming through formal channels. And it's quicker! One managing director said 'If I plant a rumour, I know that I'll get a reaction within a day. If I send a formal memo, it takes three weeks before I get a response!' Informal channels often become the only means of communication when formal channels become blocked or break down.

So if you are going to communicate effectively, you must get to understand both formal and informal channels in the network – what they are, how they work and how to use both channels to send and receive messages.

EXERCISE 1.5

What are your communication networks at work?

Work with someone else. Use A3 paper and coloured pens. Time: about 1 hour.

1. Individuals map themselves in relation to those people at work with whom they communicate: bosses, colleagues, staff, clients, suppliers, etc.

2. Show the direction of the flow of communication; use thicker lines to show heavier volume.

3. Illustrate mode of communication:

    M = formal meetings   ☎ = telephone

    ☺ = face-to-face (informal   ✉ = written letters, memos, reports,
        meetings)   etc.

4. Recheck to make sure you haven't left anyone out.

5. Put a cross against those people with whom you particularly enjoy communicating. Put a question mark against those with whom you feel uneasy or uncomfortable.

6. What is:

    (a) your dominant mode: the one you like most (see 3 above)
    (b) the greatest volume: the one you use most (why?) (see 2 above)
    (c) the direction of flow: IN → OUT (reactive)
                               OUT → IN (initiating) (see 2 above)

7. Talk things through with your partner.

8. What are your strengths and weaknesses in each mode?

Strengths	Mode	Weaknesses
well prepared	formal	you tend to make personal comments
relaxed, open-door	informal	talk too much
friendly voice	telephone	don't make notes
good, clear style	written	leave till too close to deadlines

9. What can you do to improve yourself? How?
    Be specific: set clearly measurable goals.

10. Are there any persons with whom you communicate in your job:

    (a) whom you do not like?

(b) who you feel do not think highly of you?

What are the implications:

(a) on the way you send or receive messages from them?
(b) for short-term/long-term communications?

11. Talk things through with your partner.

SUMMARY

After reading this chapter you should have a clearer picture of interpersonal communication and organizational communication: the processes, the problems and some ways to overcome these. In later chapters we will be looking at more specific applications of communication and how you can improve your effectiveness as a manager–communicator.

2

Interviewing

INTRODUCTION

We spend much of our time as managers in meeting other people – our bosses, our colleagues and our staff. On several of these occasions we have to conduct interviews. Locked into the mind of every manager is the opinion that he is a 'good' interviewer. Regrettably, in the authors' experience, this is rarely so. This chapter identifies the factors, techniques and skills that will make you a better interviewer.

An interview is defined as 'A meeting of persons face to face' and while this describes the common physical characteristic of all interview situations, it gives no indication of the many reasons why interviews are arranged. Some of those reasons are the following:

- to select a person for a specific task
- to monitor performance
- to exchange information
- to provide information
- to advise
- to counsel

and it can be seen that the control of an interview will depend very much on the reason behind it. (This concept will be dealt with in more detail in Chapter 4.)

It should already be clear that, whatever the purpose, the objective of the interview must be defined if we are to be successful. As Lewis Carroll showed in *Alice in Wonderland*:

> 'Would you tell me, please, which way I ought to go from here?'
> 'That depends a good deal on where you want to get to', said the Cat.
> 'I don't much care where . . .', said Alice.
> 'Then it doesn't matter which way you go', said the Cat.

Having defined the desired outcome of the interview – where you want to get to – you then have to decide how to achieve that end:

- decide on a suitable location;
- prepare for the interview;
- conduct the interview;
- make a judgment and analyze the results.

Location

An interview can be doomed from the start in a badly chosen location. It may be, of course, that you have no choice and that you *have* to use a specific area; this should not prevent you from organizing that area to achieve the best results.

Firstly, the location should be *comfortable*, *private* and *free from interruptions*. If there is a telephone this should be taken off the hook before the interview begins; similarly, it is a good idea to hang a 'do not disturb' sign on the door.

The room should be warm and well ventilated and lighted, so that minds will stay clear and a constructive exchange of ideas is encouraged. Seating should be comfortable and of a style compatible with the formality of the interview (it is difficult to carry out an effective disciplinary interview from easy chairs around a coffee table).

The positioning of furniture should also relate to the formality of the interview: a desk will form a physical and psychological barrier between people and should only be used for formal interviews. Where a more friendly approach is required (job interviews, performance appraisals, etc.) it is better to have informal seating without 'barriers' since this is more likely to make the interviewee feel relaxed and to provide the personal information you are seeking.

If there is a likelihood that interviewees might have to wait (and it is always difficult to specify an exact time for interviews) then it is a good idea to provide a comfortable waiting area with magazines and tea/coffee to help pass the time; where job interviews are being conducted, this is an opportunity to provide literature about the company for the interest of the interviewees.

Preparing for the interview

In all matters before beginning, a diligent preparation should be made.

Cicero

Time spent in preparation will save time, and often embarrassment, at the actual interview. The factors which need to be decided are the following:

- When is the interview to be arranged?
- How much notice should be allowed?
- How much time should be allowed?
- Who should conduct the interview?
- What questions need to be asked?
- How will the answers be recorded for future reference?
- How will interviewees be compared with each other after the interview? (If it is an interview requiring assessment.)
- What information will be given to the interviewee?

While much of the above may seem to be 'common sense', it is not unusual to find that an interviewer begins the interview with no idea of the objectives of the interview, and has not taken the time to read the relevant documents (applications etc.). This results in a disjointed and unprofessional approach by the interviewer which is not likely to impress a candidate who is there to decide whether he/she wishes to join your company.

Before the interview begins, therefore, the interviewer(s) (who should be the most suitable person(s) for the job) should always read relevant documentation and make a list of the information which needs to be obtained during the interview; this, in turn, enables specific questions to be decided and written down so that nothing will be forgotten. It also provides the basis for comparing job candidates since the interviewer(s) will have obtained the same details from each; in the same way it provides objective written information in the case of a disciplinary interview.

It is a good idea to have a standard format (with tick-boxes if you are conducting the interview(s) alone) which provides suitable headings and avoids having to write the same thing down several times (see Sample 2.1).

Conducting the interview

Conducting a successful interview requires three important skills: questioning, listening and summarizing; in addition it is necessary to make the notes referred to above.

Setting the right atmosphere for effective questioning begins with the arrival of the interviewee, at which time a few minutes should be spent in social conversation in order to provide a relaxed environment and establish a rapport between you. You need then to explain the objectives and structure of the interview, and the time allocated. Thereafter you need to proceed positively, using the right questions to obtain the information you need to achieve your objective.

Using questions for control

Questions fall into five general types, as listed below:

1. Closed questions
2. Open questions
3. Probing questions
4. Situation-related questions
5. Link questions

There are also leading questions, discriminatory questions and multiple questions which you should avoid!

Closed questions require only a yes or no answer and do not therefore result in any information other than the response to a single fact. Examples of such questions would be:

'Did you read our advertisement in *The Times*?'
'Do you have a driving licence?'

Sample 2.1 Job interview profile: administration manager

Factor requirements	Minimum requirements	Desirable
Qualifications	'A' levels: English degree Maths	Member of the Inst. of Chartered Secretaries and Administrators.
Experience	5 years in admin. job	10 years admin. experience with 5 years in senior position. Experience in a similar company or in a job-related field. Specific experience in Personnel.
Location	Living within 1 hour's travelling distance	Living within 45 minutes' travelling distance
Personal	Aged 30–40 Smart appearance Good presence and confidence Clear speaking voice Ability to deal with clients	Aged 30–35 Healthy Intellectual
Interests	Sociable and friendly with people	Actively involved in people development or has community development experience
Salary/ benefits	Earning not less than £12K	Earning £18K
Other		

Closed questions are useful for checking facts, but as the name implies, each answer 'closes' the communication until the next question is asked. While a number of closed questions may be asked in a short space of time, the interviewer would have only skeletal information about the candidate at the end. Too many closed questions also make the interviewee tend to close up – he or she will think they are being grilled!

Open questions, as you might expect, enable a breadth of information to be gathered, since they encourage the candidate to provide a fuller answer. Examples of open questions would be:

'How would your past experience help you to do this job?'

'What are your ultimate career aspirations?'

Open questions give the interviewee a good opportunity to present himself/herself, and they provide in-depth information to the interviewer who can spend more time listening to and assessing the 'whole' candidate.

Probing questions are used to gain more information about something which has already been said, possibly because a previous answer was vague or incomplete. An example could be:

'I can understand your pride in the project finishing early and below budget, but what precisely was your contribution to that?'

Probing questions provide a greater depth of knowledge about the interviewee and test the genuineness of answers already given.

Situation-related questions provide the interviewee with the opportunity to illustrate his/her skills in dealing with a particular situation. An example would be:

'How did you deal with that member of staff who was repeatedly late for work?'

This type of question enables the interviewee to show how experienced he/she is in dealing with such problems, and gives the interviewer a basis on which the quality of the answer can be compared with those of other candidates.

Link questions create a smooth logical flow in the interview. Here you form the question by picking up the last or an earlier response from the interviewee, in order to move on in a desired or different direction, such as:

'You mentioned that you were concerned about the way in which we measure inventory levels; how does this fit in with our plans for a new production control system?'

As indicated above, there are three types of questions to avoid: leading questions, discriminatory questions, and multiple questions.

Leading questions are those which 'lead' the candidate to agree with the interviewer; that is, they reveal the interviewer's own opinion so that a candidate with any sense will give the answer the interviewer wants to hear. An example of such a question would be:

'Don't you agree that managers should be really strict when dealing with bad time keeping?'

Discriminatory questions are questions which are asked of some candidates but not of others; in some cases questions of this nature could be unlawful. Examples would be:

'How would you, as an Indian Muslim, feel about working for a company which deals in meat products?' (You would not ask this same question of an English Catholic.)

'How would an attractive lady like you feel about working in the stores adjacent to the workshop?' (You would not ask this if the candidate were male.)

Multiple questions consist of a number of questions presented as a package to the interviewee. Apart from becoming confused, the interviewee tends to respond to only one question (often the 'safest' or last one), e.g. 'What was your main work in that period, how did you like it, and how does it compare with your present job?'

Listening

We have two ears and one tongue in order that we may hear more and speak less.
                                                                      Diogenes

A common fault of interviewers is their apparent readiness to launch into long monologues (well outside the need to provide basic information at the start of an interview), rather than provide the opportunity for the candidate to take part.

As a generalization, a good interviewer will not spend more than around one-third of the interview talking – which implies that for about two-thirds of the interview the interviewer will be *actively listening*.

Active listening implies much more than just hearing what is being said – it suggests that the listener will be *active* in what is being said, and will be constantly displaying attention to the interviewee. This is done in numerous ways, including:

- showing interest by looking (though not staring) at the candidate;
- smiling and nodding at appropriate times to encourage the candidate to continue with the conversation;
- resisting the temptation to allow your mind to wander on to other things.

In all forms of communication, you will find active listening to be one of the most important skills to acquire. As the Arabs say, 'If I listen, I have the advantage; if I speak, others have it.'

Summarizing

Throughout an interview, you will find that you will continually need to review or reflect on what the interviewee has said and you will also find it useful to clarify 'where you have got to' from time to time. This is done by summarizing. As the name suggests, the aim is to summarize what has been said to date to ensure that you and the candidate have the same understanding. An example of this would be:

'So, would I be correct in saying that your present job includes financial, administrative *and* personnel responsibilities?'

The great advantage of this technique is that it provides a break during which you can confirm what has already been said, you can re-target the interview and you can move into a different topic; by summarizing you can effectively curtail a verbose candidate without making him/her feel uncomfortable.

Note taking

The need for note taking has been mentioned in the previous section, and you should never rely on memory when conducting interviews relating to job applications (where a number of applicants are interviewed) or when conducting a disciplinary interview (when evidence may later have to be given to a tribunal).

Having said that, an interviewer who continually scribbles notes during an interview will undoubtedly distract the candidate and interrupt the flow of the interview. Note taking must therefore be unobtrusive and should not prevent the interviewer from listening actively. A good way is to use a pre-designed Interview Profile sheet which enables the interviewer to fill in information from documentation available before the interview, and which can be used during the interview for added data. At the end of each interview, time should be taken to write down impressions, comments, etc. so that the interview will be more easily recalled at a later date.

When an interview is likely to be complex, it is often a good idea to have a second person present to take notes, leaving the interviewer free to concentrate on the candidate. Remember, it is courteous to indicate at the beginning of the interview that you will be taking notes, to give the interviewee the opportunity to do likewise.

Closing the interview

Once you have the information you need from the interviewee, the interview can be ended, but this should be done in a way which leaves the candidate feeling comfortable. Make it clear that you have finished your questions, and give an opportunity to the candidate to put any relevant questions to you; such questions should be answered as fully and frankly as possible, bearing in mind that it is in everyone's interest that they leave the interview with a clear picture in mind.

The interviewer should then advise the candidate what the next actions are likely to be, and give some idea of the timescale involved. Finally, there are a few *don'ts* to be aware of:

- DON'T get drawn into an argument with an interviewee – you cannot possibly achieve any objective by arguing.
- DON'T allow the interviewee to take over, e.g. by asking too many questions.
- DON'T allow the candidate to waste time on any question and so prevent you from completing the interview fully.
- DON'T stay on a subject which has been answered; summarize and move on.
- DON'T intimidate a nervous candidate; give him/her a little time to relax, then proceed gently but firmly.

- DON'T be taken in by a boastful candidate; ask probing questions and get at the truth.
- DON'T arrive at an interview unprepared.
- DON'T keep an interviewee waiting; it will merely set the wrong tone for the interview from the beginning.

Making judgments and analyzing results

You may have felt, in the past, that making decisions was the most difficult part of the interviewing procedure, yet in reality it should be the easiest. By following the advice given in this chapter you will have proceeded through the following stages:

1. Deciding your objectives.
2. Planning and preparing the interview by reviewing all the information you already have, and deciding what additional information you aim to get from the interview.
3. Conducting a constructive and objective interview to enable you to obtain the facts.
4. Creating a written record of facts, observations and impressions.

You now have everything you need to make the best judgment or decision.

A selection interview

By reading through your original objectives again, you will fix them firmly in your mind; at this stage it may be worth analyzing the objectives in the light of your interviewing experience to decide if any changes need to be made.

You can then check the information you have collected against the objectives, to ascertain which candidate is the closest match to the person specification and criteria for the job.

You may feel that you should now take up any references provided by the candidate for a job interview. You should avoid references given by friends or relatives since these are unlikely to be objective; however, references from previous employers can (a) confirm information you have collected and (b) provide additional information which might give you a better picture or understanding of the candidate – particularly in respect of character, experience and suitability.

There is just one more thing left to do:

Make up your mind to act decidedly and take the consequences. No good is ever done in this world by hesitation.

Thomas Henry Huxley

EXERCISE 2.1

Consider the Situations 1 to 4 in light of the ten questions listed below:

1. How would you prepare for them?

2. How would you structure them?

3. How would you prepare for the unexpected in them?

4. What are likely to be the 'crunch' moments in the interviews?

5. How would you deal with them?

6. What outcomes will you try to achieve?

7. What will be your strategy in order to achieve them?

8. What are the worst possible outcomes?

9. How will you deal with these? Have you any contingency plans?

10. When you have worked through 1–9 above, share your thoughts with a colleague and see if he/she agrees with you.

Situation 1

You are retiring in three months' time after 12 years as departmental head. The question of your successor has been widely discussed, but no decision has been announced. You recommended to the board that your deputy for the past six years should succeed you, but have just been told that your recommendation has been ignored, and your successor (appointed from outside the company) will start next month. You have to tell your deputy that he is not to succeed you.

You would like to leave without any trouble and are prepared to do all you can to help everyone in your last few weeks. But the new man has to be run into the job, so your deputy must be made to realize that he has to help. He will remain deputy to your successor if he wishes.

Situation 2

As sales manager, you have carefully planned sales territories to minimize travelling and maximize call time. One salesman's travelling time has steadily increased beyond what you consider reasonable.

You have heard that his car is often seen outside a house in another salesman's territory. You are suspicious about what is going on, especially as your information source is usually reliable. You decide to see the salesman.

Situation 3

The production director has informed you (the works manager) that he needs a 12 per cent increase in production immediately. Your present labour force has difficulty in achieving even the present targets. Training on the job takes at least two months and interferes with production.

You therefore have no chance of achieving the increase for at least three months, and then only if you recruit and train more labour. You can work overtime and weekends, but you think this is a bad short-term solution. You decide you must see the production director and persuade him to your point of view.

Situation 4

You work in Doncaster and it is one week before the St Leger race meeting. In previous years absenteeism has been high over these three days. The board has announced, 'Anyone who cannot satisfactorily explain absence and is discovered to have gone to the races will be liable to severe disciplinary action.'

You run your accounts department semi-autonomously, and can grant occasional days off, provided that work schedules are met. However, at present, due to pressure of work, you cannot allow more than one or two people to take occasional time off at the same time.

One member of your department has asked to see you. He goes to the St Leger meeting every year but has never asked your permission before. You suspect he is going to ask for it this time. If you give him permission, you are likely to have many more requests.

Guidelines for managers for specific job-related interviews

Types of interview

When we compare the involvement and contribution of the interviewer and the interviewee, there emerge three basic types of interview: telling; telling and listening; and problem solving.

In a *telling* interview, the flow of communication is almost entirely one way – downwards. It is used most effectively in a directing, time-constrained situation; but it can cause hostility and defensive behaviour when the member of staff does not have the opportunity to participate.

In a *telling and listening* interview, more feedback from the subordinate is permitted, but the interviewer still maintains control over the flow of communication. Feelings are still not explored and the need for change may not be internalized by the interviewee.

In a *problem-solving* interview the flow of communication is two-way. The bulk of the communication is upwards, a genuine rapport is established, ideas are pooled and change facilitated.

Let us now look at some specific job situations and consider how managers should approach them, bearing in mind the types of interviews described above.

Problem-solving interviews

Here the member of staff has at least an equal interest in a successful outcome. Although major responsibility for the presentation and conduct is likely to rest with the interviewer, the member of staff also needs to prepare and to accept some responsibility for what occurs. He/she may also need help and should be encouraged to:

- Appreciate the purpose of the interview.
- Express his/her own views, and back them up with facts and examples wherever possible.
- Regard the interview as a problem-solving meeting.
- Appreciate the boss's problems in his/her job and in his/her role at the interview: to be tolerant, but get his/her points across.

- Clarify uncertainties.
- Agree priorities for future action.

Attitude rules for the interviewer

1. Give your whole attention to the person you are interviewing and make it evident that you are doing so.

2. Do not display any kind of authority.

3. Never argue; never give advice.

4. Listen to what the person:
   (a) wants to say;
   (b) does not want to say;
   (c) cannot say without your help.

5. Talk or ask questions only for the following reasons:
   (a) help the person talk;
   (b) relieve fears or anxieties;
   (c) summarize what has been said and present for verification or comment;
   (d) clarify;
   (e) steer the discussion towards some topic that is being avoided.

6. Give attention to issues of confidentiality and obtain agreement about the circumstances in which you can discuss them.

Procedure rules

1. State the problem, not the answer.

2. Identify the key facts in the situation.

3. Restate the problem in terms of the conditions which should exist when the problem is resolved.

4. List the obstacles to achieving the conditions (or objectives) which are sought.

5. List possible solutions, i.e. ways of overcoming the obstacles, *without evaluation*.

6. Agree criteria for deciding which will be the best.

7. Discuss solutions.

8. Select best solutions.

9. Agree implementation programme:
   (a) who does what, when, how;
   (b) what form of feedback/monitoring;
   (c) what difficulties can be expected and what preventive/correct-ive action will be necessary.

Delegation interviews

In every joint work-planning and joint problem-solving discussion between a manager and his/her subordinate, issues over delegation are bound to occur. In essence, delegation is about trust. It involves judgment about whether someone else has the ability to make decisions and take action on your behalf and is ready to do so.

Various stages of delegation suggest themselves which can be roughly linked to interviewing styles:

1. No involvement No delegation	Orders are issued, no explanation is given, strict compliance expected.	'Tell'
2. No delegation Some information shared	Orders are given and the reasons are explained.	'Tell and sell'
3. No delegation More information shared	The problem/situation is explained and also alternative solutions. Orders are then given.	
4. Some participation First stage in delegation	The problem is outlined and subordinates asked to suggest solutions which are discussed. The decision is made for them.	'Tell and listen'
5. Controlled delegation More participation	The problem is presented, subordinates' solutions are discussed. The senior indicates his preference, leaves the decision to the subordinates, but asks to be informed of what has been decided.	

6. Delegation with marginal control	As above, but senior does not indicate preferred solution.	
7. Full involvement Full delegation	The subordinates get the problem to solve on their own. *They* decide when to report back (i.e. when *they* think it is appropriate and this will normally be after all necessary action has been taken and results are beginning to show).	'Joint problem solving'

Remember when delegating, you must set up monitoring systems to ensure that performance standards are being maintained.

Disciplinary interviews

Attitudes
Employees like:

- to know in advance which rules and regulations will apply;
- to have a say in formulating the rules under which they will work;
- to have an opportunity to change existing rules when they feel they are no longer appropriate.

Employees want:

- to know in advance what action will be taken when they violate a rule;
- a fair hearing when they have been accused of rule violation.

Preparation
- Do I have *all* the facts?
- Do I have direct evidence or am I basically dealing with other people's opinions, circumstantial evidence or conjecture?
- What other people are involved, directly or indirectly?
- Am I certain I have the complete picture of what happened?

The employee
- Have I talked to the employee in private?

- Did I give him a fair chance to present his/her side of the situation?
- What is the employee's overall record – length of service, performance, behaviour?
- To what extent was the employee familiar with the rules or regulations? Should he/she have been expected to know?
- Did the employee have fair warning of the possible consequences of his/her action?
- Are there any unusual circumstances, personal or otherwise, that must be considered in this case?

Action

- To what extent has this rule been enforced in the past?
- Is the action I am considering consistent with that applied in prior situations?
- Is the action appropriate in view of the infraction?
- What impact might the action have on (a) the employee concerned, (b) other employees?
- Am I handling this in a fair and impartial way?
- Am I prepared to explain *why* my action is necessary?
- Will the action prevent a recurrence of the employee's behaviour in the future?

Preventing insubordination

Few situations can be more threatening to managers than an employee's refusal to do a job or carry out an order, particularly if they think they are unlikely to be supported by their seniors when they take 'firm' action. Often, however, they themselves contribute to the act of refusal, because they are insufficiently sensitive to the employee's feelings which are usually very strong before he or she will take such a stand. Such feelings are particularly likely to arise over the allocation of tasks considered to be degrading.

When sensing that resistance is likely to be encountered, a manager might consider the following:

- the importance of asking an employee in private to do a job;
- reacting to feelings, such as feeling that the work is degrading;

- recognizing that privileges allocated on a seniority basis may not be popular;
- the need to delve deeper into the situation when the feelings expressed do not seem adequate to account for behaviour;
- exploring the possibility that the problem arose because of relationships within the work group and might therefore be a group, rather than an individual, problem;
- appreciating that both parties – the manager as well as the employee – might be involved in a face-saving situation.

Handling reprimands

A reprimand is an occurrence requiring (a) disciplinary action and (b) guidance action. Most organizations have clearly defined codes of conduct (usually set out in a rule book). The aims of a reprimand should be to (a) improve work performance, (b) prevent recurrence of offences, and (c) protect others from careless or dangerous behaviour.

Suggested ways of dealing with reprimands

1. Preparation
    (a) Make sure you have *facts*.
    (b) If necessary, take time to investigate as fully as possible.
    (c) Plan as far as possible what you will say and do in relation to the individual concerned. What is mild to one is very severe to another.

Remember: if you are not in possession of the facts, the effects of your reprimand could be damaging: to yourself, the individual concerned and the organization. Arbitrary managerial action causes serious repercussions today.

2. Interview
    (a) Ensure privacy. Never reprimand in public.
    (b) Be rational. Keep control of yourself and of the interview.
    (c) Go straight to the point. It is stressful for the individual to approach a reprimand obliquely.
    (d) Be precise and exact about the offence. Do not drag in anything other than the immediate issue.

(e) Do not allow yourself to be dragged into an argument, but be prepared to allow an opportunity for a full reply from the individual.

(f) Do not accept justification or excuses. If you have discovered the *facts*, there can be only mitigating circumstances.

(g) Together, work out ways of improving performance and/or behaviour that fits the workplace rules, customs and practices.

3. Check results

Immediately afterwards, make a note of what you expect to happen. This enables you to check performance. Once the reprimand is over, do not harbour resentment or display any antagonism.

Handling grievances

People can become irritated by many things at work, from unpleasant working conditions to personal frictions. These can give rise to *grievances*. Most organizations have grievance procedures, which generally name the immediate workgroup supervisor as the first stage. In the United Kingdom, this is a legal requirement.

Whether grievances are real or imaginary, justified or unjustified is usually less important than the aggrieved's attitude. It is important, therefore, that managerial responses to grievances should be rational. The following is a suggested way of dealing with a grievance interview:

1. Put the person at ease. This is best done by showing you are prepared to listen.

2. Listen carefully. You may need to be patient, as people often conceal their real grievance until they see something of your reactions.

3. Ask searching questions: who, why, what, when, where, which: until you are satisfied you have identified the real causes of the grievance.

4. Restate what you have identified and try to agree that this is accurate.

5. Do not evade the issues, even if they hurt.

6. Seek to establish agreement on what should be done, both by you and the aggrieved.

7.   Never make promises you cannot keep.

8.   Even if the grievance is invalid, be rational. Ensure the aggrieved realizes he/she can always talk to you. If you feel your time is being wasted, are you in the right job? People need to talk – even if they have very little to say.

When you have finished the interview, note for yourself what you expect to see happen. This provides you with a performance check.

Handling promotion issues

The way decisions about promotion are made and announced can have a bearing on the degree of acceptance or non-acceptance of the decisions. The criteria used are often not clear or not stated, and there will obviously be different views about the importance of seniority and personal acceptability, and the job requirements.

If managers and supervisors try to learn beforehand the type of reaction that different promotions might produce they may be able to prevent major dissatisfaction and morale problems from arising. Much hinges on the way they conduct interviews, whether they are prepared to explore other people's viewpoints and discover the nature of any objections that may be around.

What commonly happens is that the supervisor allows himself/herself to fall into a 'tell and sell' situation. He/she presents the decision, tells the person who has been passed over about his/her weaknesses and tries to justify the decision. The result is almost certain to create hostility and defensiveness, and since the objections are not likely to be disclosed, they are not likely to be overcome.

Handling overtime issues

Overtime could be described as one of the potential flash-points in industrial relations. Although management attitudes and action will clearly influence the climate, the real key to the correct handling of overtime lies in the method and style adopted by the manager. The following points may help to provide guidelines:

1.   Insisting on management's 'right' to demand overtime is not likely to be productive.

2. From the employees' viewpoint it is the company's job to forecast consumer demand and budget adequately for production short-falls. They need to be convinced that you have done all you can to avoid overtime in your approach to work organization.

3. When considering who works the overtime, you will naturally prefer to use the people most competent and experienced, but your demand may cause considerable inconvenience as you may be in conflict with domestic demands.

4. Overtime rates are usually pitched at an attractive level. To work overtime may therefore be regarded as a 'perk' and you may have to ensure an even distribution of overtime working among the work force. This may mean you have to use less effective people.

5. Try to give notice as far ahead as possible and see that unpopular periods are fairly allocated.

6. Customs and practices – precedents – get established over many years and people may be reluctant to accept change. You may have to work hard to get new ideas accepted.

7. If you ask people to work overtime, they must be clear about what tasks they have to perform, who else will be working, and how the work will be supervised.

Handling work groups: group decisions

Here we outline a four-step procedure which a manager can use when he has had some experience with group discussions and is ready to learn some refinements.

- *Step one: Studying the problem* is the preparation period and deals with analyzing the setting of the problem and the manager's attitude.

- *Step two: Sharing the problem* deals with the manner in which the problem is presented and will greatly determine whether the employees react constructively or become defensive.

- *Step three: Discussing the problem* is concerned with discussion procedures and the manager's responsibilities for conducting a discussion.

- *Step four: Solving the problem* deals with the objectives for obtaining acceptance of a solution.

47

These steps need not be taken as a strict sequence, although in general they do serve that purpose. In practice you may wish to reverse the process, and procedures must in any case be adapted to suit your own personality and style.

Step 1: studying the problem

1. Check your responsibility: how does the problem involve your responsibility and authority?
   (a) is it within your own area of freedom?
   (b) should it be discussed first with your boss?
   (c) should it go 'higher up the line'?
   (d) what is your responsibility towards units at the same level as yours?
   (e) what constraints are there from wage considerations or union agreements?

2. Check your attitude:
   (a) are you willing to encourage the group to solve the problem?
   (b) will you get the group to consider long-term results?
   (c) will you respect the views of everyone in the group?
   (d) do you think the group *can* solve the problem?
   (e) will you accept a solution different from the one you had in mind?

3. Plan your presentation: is there a problem because:
   (a) production is suffering?
   (b) employees are violating rules?
   (c) your boss is raising the problem?
   (d) morale is poor?
   (e) some other reason?

Step 2: sharing the problem

1. State the problem:
   (a) present it in positive terms rather than fault-finding terms;
   (b) state the problem in such a manner that there is mutual interest;
   (c) make the statement so that it stimulates interest and avoids giving rise to defensive reactions.

2. Provide essential information:
   (a) present the facts;
   (b) if opinions are important, label them as opinions;

(c) check that your approach is not biased by a preconceived solution;

(d) get additional facts during the meeting if you need them: no face will be lost.

Step 3: discussing the problem

1. Encourage free discussion:
   (a) establish an atmosphere which enables everyone to have a say without criticism;
   (b) let members of the group do most of the talking and answering each other;
   (c) avoid stepping into the discussion and ruling out some idea that looks impossible: let the group do it.

2. Get everyone to participate:
   (a) ask quiet people for their views;
   (b) avoid putting people 'on the spot';
   (c) try to develop an attitude in the group that each person has the responsibility for giving his or her views.

3. Keep discussion on the point:
   (a) individuals need to feel free to talk about many things, but this does not imply wide digression;
   (b) the group should experience progress: wide digressions prevent this;
   (c) distinguish between the need for controlling digressions and dominating the discussion.

4. Respect minority opinions:
   (a) failure to respect minority views leads to opting out;
   (b) good ideas are often minority ones;
   (c) minority views are often hostile.

Step 4: solving the problem

1. The solution is a meeting of minds:
   (a) it grows out of the group;
   (b) it is not a voting process, where majority rules;
   (c) it may be one that no individual held at the outset.

2. The leader should summarize and check for group agreement:
   (a) summarizing indicates progress and clarifies the issues;

(b) as points are summarized the group feels that it has arrived at a basis for exploring the problem further;

(c) checking for agreement allows expression of individual attitudes;

(d) summarizing gives the group a chance to learn who is for and who is against. This reveals differences that remain as problems.

3. The solution should specify action:

(a) not only *what* should be done, but *when* and *how*.

4. The group should be able to reopen the subject:

(a) errors may not emerge until the solution is tried;
(b) decisions are not made for all time;
(c) the group may not get the best answer first time.

Performance management

The work contract
It must be set out clearly so that employees:

1. Know the overall nature of the work they have to do: tasks, activities, accountabilities.
2. Have clear information about what they are expected to achieve in terms of quality standards, output and cost constraints.
3. Have, or have easy access to, the materials, tools and facilities to perform the job required.
4. Know what they can and cannot decide for themselves.
5. Know what results they are achieving.
6. Understand how the pay for their work is determined and what benefits they can expect, e.g. sick pay, holidays, bonus.

Work planning and review
To contribute effectively to the management of people at work, the manager needs to follow the points specified below:

1. Be informed about and understand the total situation of his unit and the organization as a whole.
2. Be clear about the tasks people have to perform and their interrelationship with other tasks and functions.

3. Understand what can and cannot be measured.

4. Know how to evaluate results against standards.

5. Follow a joint problem-solving approach to work planning, work review and performance appraisal.

6. Involve employees either individually or in groups in planning any changes in their work – well in advance of the event.

7. Try progressively to delegate authority to make decisions and decrease the points that have to be referred upwards.

8. Involve employees, probably through representatives, in planning, implementing and monitoring the systems which affect or control their work (e.g. safety, rules, grievance procedures, training, overtime).

9. See that employees get help or guidance when they need it.

Training needs interviews

1. Discuss with the job holder the activities that comprise his/her job and ascertain the degree of authority he/she has to make decisions. Seek his/her views on improvements.

2. Examine with the job holder the problems he/she meets at work – both tasks and relationships. Agree on what action is required.

3. Agree performance standards with the job holder.

4. Discuss knowledge/information and skill requirements. Agree methods of gaining improvements.

5. See yourself primarily as someone who creates opportunities to learn and makes facilities available.

Exit interviews

It is essential that management learn and understand the *real* reasons why people leave their organizations. Without this information, no action can be taken to prevent others doing the same. The reasons can be many:

- poor pay
- poor boss–subordinate relationships
- poor colleague relationships

- poor working environment
- lack of promotion opportunities
- no challenge in the job
- no rewards for achievement etc.

The interview should be carried out on problem-solving lines, and requires considerable skills to elicit the information from the employee, who may be aggrieved with you and the organization. Therefore:

- Put the leaver at ease.
- Keep an open mind.
- Ask open-ended questions, but never argue or advise.
- Listen to:
  what the person wants to say; what he/she does not want to say; and what he/she cannot say without help.
- Mirror or reflect the leaver's views: clarify, summarize, but do not twist or add to what he/she says.
- Go at the leaver's own speed.
- Keep the process going, even in the face of anxiety or hostility.
- Learn to recognize and accept your own feelings – do not try to escape from them, but learn to deal with them and those of the leaver sensitively.

SUMMARY

We have identified that, in any interview situation, the objective of the interview must be known and understood by both parties. Interview success will occur only if suitable preparation is made by the interviewer and interviewee, rapport established early in the interview, and control exercised by the effective use of questions by the interviewer. Guidelines have been given for managers dealing with specific incidents and situations at work.

Here's to your next interview!

3

Making presentations

'Where shall I begin, please your Majesty?' he asked. 'Begin at the beginning', the King said, gravely, 'and go on till you come to the end: then stop.'

Lewis Carroll, *Alice in Wonderland*

INTRODUCTION

This advice was given to the White Rabbit, and in many ways it is exactly the advice needed when considering the making of a presentation. How you begin, what comes in the middle and how you end probably does not seem as simple as the King's advice, but the following chapter will provide you with the necessary information to enable you to give an effective speech or presentation.

The purposes for making presentations are many, but can be grouped in the following way:

1. To demonstrate: a service, product, system.
2. To create: an image, strategy.
3. To entertain: colleagues, outside people.
4. To sell: a concept, product, idea.
5. To represent: a group, company, department.
6. To promote: an attitude, a way of working.
7. To suggest: a solution, a new concept.

No matter what the reason for the presentation, it should always be remembered that what you are consistently seeking is the promotion of better communication, the most professional standards of presentation, and the commitment to greater awareness of the needs of others.

However good you are on your feet, you are unlikely to be successful unless you have prepared thoroughly. For any presentation, the first thing to consider is, 'What are my objectives?' Be sure you know why you are making the presentation and what you want from it. When structuring the presentation, check that the basic steps help you achieve the overall objective.

There are five stages to consider for a successful presentation:

1. Set your objective.
2. Plan the presentation.
3. Prepare the materials.
4. Rehearse and practise.
5. Be ready and prepared on the day.

No two situations are the same, but whatever the situation, success will not be achieved unless you follow some basic rules and have asked yourself some basic questions. Knowing to whom you are actually making the presentation is one of the most fundamental questions to be asked. Exercise 3.1 deals with a list of questions you should consider when *planning* your presentation.

EXERCISE 3.1 PLANNING

What is your audience's background?
How knowledgeable are they?
What are their strengths and weaknesses?
How can your ideas be of benefit/threat to them?
What should your appearance be?
What is your status in relation to your audience?
Is there some common ground?
What impression do you want to create?
Have all aspects of the idea been considered?
What specific points need emphasizing?
What are the possible objections?
Where will you be required to make the presentation?
What date and what time of day?
How many people will be attending?
Are there other speakers? If so, what will they be speaking about?
Where in the sequence of events do you fit in?
Will you need AVA facilities? Microphone? Can you use a microphone well?
Will you be expected to provide handouts etc.?

Timing is an extremely important point. You must know how long you are expected to talk so that you can prepare and rehearse what you have to say. It is also good to know at what time of day your presentation is to be made as this will help you to decide what kind of 'mood' the audience is likely to be in.

When rehearsing, you will probably find that you will overrun or underrun, and therefore you can change the structure of your presentation to conform with your allocated time. One guideline you can use is that the introduction and summary should take up only 20 per cent of your presentation time, leaving the other 80 per cent for the main subject matter, as shown in Figure 3.1. Sections A to E in the figure are amplified below:

A. Introduction and objectives, reasons for the presentation (10% of time available).

    An introduction should be short, snappy and catch the audience's attention. This is a critical period in which you should be trying to establish a rapport with the audience. They have a choice of listening or not – you must motivate them to want to listen.

B. Introduction of main themes, issues (20% of time available).

    Here you identify and explain the basic themes and issues concerning your presentation, the key elements you wish to develop.

C. Development of main themes, issues (40% of time available).

    You develop your arguments logically and rationally, showing clearly the relationship between the themes and arguments.

D. Integration of main themes, issues (20% of time available).

    Here you pull together the main themes of your presentation. Do not introduce any new themes at this stage – it will only lead to confusion.

E. Summary or conclusion (10% of time available).

    The message you want to leave with the audience is encapsulated here. You must be clear what your objectives are, to ensure that the message, the reason for giving the presentation, gets across. Summarize the main points; pull together all loose ends; and stress the way in which your argument leads to your required conclusion. End on a high note – and thank the audience for listening: they did not have to, even if they were coerced into attending!

You will need to consider the *facilities* – where you will be making your presentation, how the room will be set out – and what *equipment* is available at

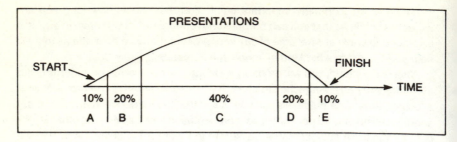

Figure 3.1 Structuring a presentation

the venue, and whether the equipment you wish to use can be used effectively in the room allocated. Showing OHP slides on a wall with a fairly bold pattern is not conducive to good attention or the credibility of the presenter!

Make sure that your presentation suits the audience to whom you are presenting, and make sure that there is adequate formality for the individual groups. Do not assume that what is good enough for a small group of colleagues will work just as effectively with a group of fifty people from all other departments within your organization.

Preparation

David Niven once said, when making a speech, 'Tonight I feel like Zsa Zsa Gabor's fifth husband. I know what to do but how do I make it interesting?'

In any presentation, it is only you the speaker who know the exact nature of the material you are about to deliver. To ensure that you get the information across in the best manner you need to consider the following points:

1. It is vitally important that you research and prepare the information. Once you have decided what you want to communicate, you need to collect all the information required to do the job effectively. A great deal of the information will already be stored in your mind, so that should be written down first, and then other details added as you acquire the additional data.

2. The information should be presented in a logical and sequential manner to ensure that the audience understand the events, are

able to reach some solution to the problem, or are left with a clear understanding of the reason for the presentation. A natural order to your presentation makes listening easier for the audience and makes the presentation easier to remember.

3. It is necessary to give all the required information, as gaps tend to present problems. If the presentation is difficult to follow because of the lack of information, the audience will lose the thread of the message and lose interest. It is often said that a presentation is like a string of beads, with the beads linked by a logical thread.

4. The opening and closing section of the presentation are as important as the middle part. Bob Monkhouse, in his book *Just Say a Few Words*, says that 'in the beginning is the hook . . . the means of grabbing the crowd.' A striking introduction is a useful way to achieve a good presentation, providing that the rest of the material follows suit. The opening statement should say what you want to communicate and the closing statement should be a summary so that everyone is clear about what you have achieved.

EXERCISE 3.2 PREPARATION CHECKLIST

When you have planned your presentation, examine the following:

1. Objectives: recheck that you have defined your objective correctly.

2. Structure: does your presentation have a clearly identifiable structure?

3. Content: is all said that needs saying?

4. Sequence: is it logical? Are all links and summaries appropriate?

5. Time: is sufficient time available for all you want to say?

6. Balance: is each section weighted correctly? Check the priorities of your arguments and facts.

7. Conclusion: does it make people sit up and agree with you? Is it punchy?

8. Objectives: do all the above work towards achieving your objectives?

Practice and rehearsal are essential if you wish to develop the necessary skills to be a good presenter. Some people prefer to practise away from everyone else, in a distant room with just a mirror to represent the audience, whereas others will perform to a sympathetic friend/colleague/spouse and require some constructive criticism. Another method is to tape the presentation and to listen to it a few times, thus allowing you to make any necessary or desirable changes.

When you are rehearsing, don't do your presentation sub-vocally, or simply read it in your mind. You must recite it, stop where you have problems and start again from there. If you do not speak it aloud, your timing will be all wrong. Remember also that it will take longer on the day, so do not try to cram too much into the time available.

EXERCISE 3.3 DEVELOPING PRESENTATION SKILLS

Prepare a short presentation to last five minutes. Your audience are your colleagues, and the subject matter is about something that you have a deep interest in or about which you hold a strong conviction.

Tape your presentation and listen to it, making notes about changes you would make. Leave the tape for a few days and listen to it again, making any new changes you feel you wish to make. Ask a friend or colleague to listen and make comments.

Compare notes and then repeat the taping, making all changes you and your colleague have suggested.

When making the actual presentation you must be aware of the attitudes you may have to face and the techniques you can use to help you make the best presentation you can.

Where attitudes are concerned you must have a good understanding of your audience, their motivations and their perceptions of you. The types of audience you may be faced with are: your superiors; your colleagues; your team; a mixed audience; a hostile audience; an international audience.

Your superiors: although this may sound a little daunting, you have the expertise, a given amount of time and the knowledge that they need to know about the content of your presentation. To ensure a good presentation you must be thoroughly prepared, accurate, concise, positive, honest and assertive.

Your colleagues: it is possible that this audience could prove to be one of your most difficult. In many organizations there is a certain amount of rivalry between departments. They may resent any ideas or changes that you are presenting to them. In this situation you should strive to be prepared and know the facts, be natural and assertive, avoid aggressive statements and being overly protective towards your own department, and know your strengths and work to them rather than trying to oversell the points you are making.

Your team: they will probably behave differently in a formal situation than in normal day-to-day business meetings. They will certainly expect that any presentation should show preparation, knowledge, authority and confidence. If you treat your team with friendliness and sincerity, you should be able to present ideas to them in an informal, intelligent and, possibly, an entertaining way.

A mixed audience: the 'what, why and how' audience, because often you are not aware of what they already know, what they actually want to hear, why they have been invited to the presentation and how, if at all, they relate to each other. Thus you may be unsure about the level at which to pitch your presentation, what amount of knowledge to assume, what kind of language to use, and from what particular angle to approach the subject. Consider the following:

1. Keep things simple, explicit, clear (the 'Kiss' syndrome – Keep It Simple Stupid!).

2. Avoid jargon, private jokes or in-words.

3. Allow the audience to know that you know that they are from various backgrounds and that some of your presentation may be familiar to some of them.

4. Create a sense of common purpose.

5. Try to present your material from different angles.

A hostile audience: you may be faced with this kind of audience for many reasons and the audience could either be people you know well or hardly at all. Knowing the subject thoroughly and having all the vital information as back-up material will prove invaluable. If you use the time allocated to the full, you will find that it will be appreciated by the audience regardless of their feelings about the content.

An international audience: 'any effective speaker must learn to adapt a talk according to the expectations of his audience', states Robert Moran in an article entitled 'Tips on making speeches to international audiences'. He lists many cultural differences to be taken into consideration: Japanese audiences look for sincerity through an indirect approach with ambiguities throughout and a careful exploration of inner meanings; French audiences need statements to be substantiated and opinions supported with numbers and facts; Americans favour practical questions to explore how things work in practice; German audiences tend to focus on technical aspects, so all figures must be exact; Swedish audiences tend to pose theoretical questions and seek to define the strategies mentioned in the presentation.

All the points mentioned return to the fact that you must find out all you can about your audience. You want their explicit agreement to listen and you have to use your personality, your introduction to the subject and your preparation to ensure that this is gained. In agreeing to listen they admit that you probably have something worthwhile to say. Where it is appropriate, involve them in the communication by participation: inviting questions, ideas and views from your audience.

Being enthusiastic about the subject of your presentation will often be passed on to your audience. Some people believe that enthusiasm, like laughter, is infectious. The important point is that the person who really believes in what he or she is saying, and enjoys it, will instil the same feeling in the listener.

Be sincere: if an audience feels that the information being presented is not complete or is misleading, then its response may be to take the opposite viewpoint. You should believe in the information you are presenting. Making eye contact with your audience is one way to present a sincere image, providing that you do not glare consistently at one person or at one side of the audience. Moving your eyes around the audience will make everyone feel involved.

If you are not used to making presentations, you may be tempted to copy someone else's style. However, there is only one Tom Peters, and although his presentation style can be described as 'bizarre', only he could carry it off so well. You must use your own natural abilities and skills and be yourself. Be natural and straightforward and that will work for you in the most positive way.

Presentation techniques

The techniques which can help to ensure a successful presentation are concerned with: the words you use; your appearance; the use of your voice; body language; using notes; visual aids; and answering questions.

The words you use

It is often said that no matter how good the presentation may be, or how smart and attractive your appearance, or how dynamic your visual aids, it is, in the final analysis, what you say that actually matters.

Words are the main vehicle for making your communication, so your objective should be to talk clearly, concisely, intelligibly and in an enthusiastic, interesting and motivating way.

Visual aids are important to enhance the points you are making, but you should also try to create the image through your use of words. Use examples, analogies and word pictures to give interesting and graphic illustrations to your points. Most people are able to visualize and understand more easily from an example than from a technical description.

EXAMPLE 3.1

At a presentation on the benefits of a training course which used video as a means of enhancing future performances, the presenter stated accurately that 'the course uses video to aid personal presentation skills'. The reaction was one of mild interest. When he looked at his own presentation and talked to colleagues about improving his performance, he realized that he needed to be more enthusiastic. The next time he was 'selling' the course he changed his statement to 'the video is used effectively. You can actually see yourself perform as others really see you!' This conjured up the image in everyone's brain of actually performing and watching afterwards.

Avoid the use of expressions like 'um', 'er', 'you know', 'you see'. Many of us use these without really being aware, but they can be distracting, especially if they are used excessively. If you do use any of these constantly then you must make every effort to stop using them. Instead, pause and collect your thoughts, look at your notes, take a deep breath. Any of these would be more acceptable to your audience.

Talking to people who do not have the same amount of expertise as yourself means that the words you use should be jargon-free and free from all technical terms which are likely to be unknown. You should also avoid slang and colloquialisms as these are often open to misinterpretation. The audience is not there to unravel verbal puzzles, so keep your words simple and easy to understand.

Your appearance

People make instant assumptions from the visual contacts they make. You will not necessarily be judged by your appearance, but how your presentation is received will be determined by how you present yourself. Points to consider are:

— you should be dressed comfortably which means avoiding tight-fitting, brand-new and heavy clothing.

— whatever you decide to wear should be right for the occasion. Jeans and jumper would not be a good idea when making a presentation to potential clients, and a formal dinner suit or evening gown may be too extreme for the afternoon presentation to a society group.

— make sure that whatever you wear is neat, tidy and clean. Making the time to check on your appearance just before you start your presentation can alert you to any problems.

— try not to wear anything which could prove to be too distracting, or perfume or aftershave which is too overpowering.

— if you are the type of person who fidgets with 'things' then avoid having anything about your person which will encourage the habit!

The use of your voice

The way you use your voice can help to put across a controlled, interesting, rational and comprehensive message. The points you should consider are: volume, tone, pitch, speed, and breathing.

Volume: the first aim of any speaker is to be heard, so adapt the loudness of your voice to the size of the audience, the size and acoustic qualities of the room and the emphasis you wish to use on certain words. You do not have to shout to be understood, but speaking up allows you to communicate more clearly.

Tone: speaking in a monotone is very boring to the listener. You can use your tone for emphasis, effect and to signal a break or link. When you raise your voice slightly, you appear to be increasing the intensity of feeling that you put into those particular words. Speaking more softly will tend to increase audience concentration.

Pitch: changing the pitch of your voice often indicates to the audience that you have finished with one particular point and that you are about to go on to the next. Pitch change can also give a dramatic effect.

Speed: speaking at one constant speed can be as off-putting as talking in a monotone. You will need to practise speeding up and slowing down as you speak. It is better if you can begin your presentation slowly because you will speed up as you get into your presentation. A pause can be used to good effect because it can create anticipation and encourage attention. The summaries should be done slowly, remembering that for most of the people the information is new and therefore they need time to absorb it.

Breathing: nervousness can cause your breathing to be irregular and erratic. It is a good exercise for your own self-confidence to know that you are quite capable of getting through your longest paragraph without gasping at the end. Should you find that you are getting short of breath, you will become more nervous, flustered and getting more short of breath which will make you more nervous . . .. If you should find that this is happening, then it is better to take an unscheduled deep breath than to flounder on.

EXERCISE 3.4 THE USE OF YOUR VOICE

Look back at your last presentation when you are preparing for your next one, and consider:

1. Is your voice boring?

2. Do you speak in a monotone, or vary your pitch?

3. Is the speed of your delivery constant? Varied?

4. Do you drop your voice at the end of a sentence?

5. Is your breathing right? Do you run out of breath in the middle of a sentence? (It's probably too long then!)

6. How do you make a point or emphasize a key issue? Do you raise your voice? Do you speak more slowly? More quickly? Do you repeat it?

7. Do you use long words? Short words? Long sentences? Why? When?

8. Are your words within the vocabulary of your audience? Do they understand you?

9. After your next presentation, ask a friend in the audience for constructive feedback on the above points.

Body language

The use of non-verbal communication can lead to greater effectiveness. To counteract the nervousness that you will probably feel, stand straight and tall. You will not only look confident, but you will feel more confident also. Make sure that you do not slouch, that you do not exaggerate movements which will prove to be distracting and that you can control any habits that others would find intolerable. Do not be afraid to use gestures, but do make sure that they are natural. Watching yourself on a video can highlight many of these points.

Your facial expressions will be mirrored by your audience. If you look serious your audience will feel the same and reflect that feeling back to you. If you find it difficult to use gestures and still feel natural, try to let your feeling and your meaning be mirrored in your expression. This will make it easier for your audience to relate to your message. A dead-pan expression is very off-putting, so it is important to remember to smile! A smile will bring warmth to your presentation and will also help to create a friendly atmosphere and rapport with your audience.

EXERCISE 3.5 YOUR BODY LANGUAGE

How do you use your body to communicate during a presentation?

1.   Do you talk to the audience, or to the screen behind you?

2.   Do you actively seek eye contact with specific members of the audience? Do you sweep over them or fix them beadily in the eye?

3.   Do you know who the decision makers are, and speak primarily to them?

4.   Do you tend to concentrate on looking to the right or left, to the front or back of the audience?

5.   Are your gestures congruent with your message? Too exaggerated? Are you too stiff?

6.   Do you have any distracting mannerisms?

7.   Do you point at the audience? Wag your finger?

8.   Are your movements simple? Or do you pace like a caged tiger?

9.   Are you natural? Are you yourself?

10.   Do you create barriers between you and your audience?

Before you make your next presentation, consider the points above, and how you can best use body language to reinforce your message.

After your next presentation, ask a friend in the audience for feedback on your body language.

Using notes

It is always helpful to have notes on the main points summarized on some sort of card. A good exercise is to start off by writing the whole presentation down, and then as you practise and become more accustomed to the presentation, you can condense it into succinct headings. You must make sure that your notes are legible and can be good indicators of your next point.

Using a different colour pen or a highlighter to alert you to making a change in your tone or pitch, to pause or to make a gesture, will help with the final presentation. These points can only be made by recording your presentation and listening to it and making the changes where necessary. Do not use floppy sheets of A4 paper for your notes: put them on to small cards which you can hold in one hand and refer to, and make sure you have them in the correct sequence before you start. Number the cards, and tie them together with a piece of string through the top left hand corners. If you don't, and you drop the loose cards, you'll never find your sequence again!

Visual aids

They are as they suggest, an aid to communication. They must be relevant, simple and bold. You do have options when presenting things by means of aids. In particular:

- You do not *have* to use audio or visual aids.
- Try to assess the value of all the aids you can use before making your decision.
- If you mix your media try to match the various formats.
- Ask yourself why you want to use aids and what you hope to achieve.

When aids are used properly they can arouse interest, show visually things that are difficult to describe verbally, focus interest on key points, and provide clarity of understanding as the senses are combined to absorb the matter presented. The more interesting you can make your illustrations, the more chance there is that you will capture your audience's attention. Be sure that you restrict the information on each aid to only one point. If there are a number of different points you want to illustrate, use one aid for each.

Be careful that you do not stand in front of your visual aids: your audience cannot see through you! Allow sufficient time for your audience to absorb the information and then remove it from view and go on to the next point.

EXERCISE 3.6 VISUAL AIDS CHECKLIST

1. Do your visual aids reinforce points you have made or are making?

2. Keep quiet while your audience studies the aid – they won't listen until they've read it.

3. When you have made your point with the aid, remove it before you move forward.

4. **When using an OHP:**
    (a) look at the audience, not at the screen – glance at the projector to check where you are;
    (b) to emphasize a point, use a pointer on the projector, not the screen – you'll lose audience contact otherwise;
    (c) make sure everyone can see the screen;
    (d) your writing must be large enough to be legible by the audience at the back;
    (e) make sure the lamp on the OHP is working before you start the presentation, and that you have a spare bulb;
    (f) check your slide is central before switching on;
    (g) turn off OHP between slides;
    (h) make sure your slides are in the correct sequence before the presentation.

5. **When using a whiteboard:**
    (a) check that the available pens are not dry;
    (b) keep your pens in your spare hand, keep them in the same sequence, e.g. black, red, blue, green, and return them to that position when you have used them;
    (c) after using a pen, always replace the cap;

(d) try not to turn your back on the audience when writing. Stand to the *right* of your writing, facing the right of your audience, and move towards the left of your audience when writing, exposing the writing as you go.

6. **When using a flipchart:**

(a) if you have already prepared your flipcharts, make sure they are in the right sequence;

(b) flipcharts never seem to come apart singly when you want them to: fold up one bottom corner of each – it will make it so much easier;

(c) if you have not prepared your flipcharts, and you are going to write your message/points as you go, cheat! Write your points faintly in pencil on the chart and then just go over it in pen. This is especially effective when you are drawing a picture or diagram – people will think you are Rolf Harris!

(d) keep your pens in sequence, as for using a whiteboard.

Answering questions

You must listen to the questions carefully and answer them as straightforwardly as possible. It is rather rude to tell a questioner that the question is stupid or was covered by the presentation. Try to empathize with the person, and realize that you may have to make a point much clearer to answer the particular question.

How you introduce the question session has a large impact on how it will develop. Asking gruffly, 'So, are there any questions?' is likely to deter the audience from participating. If you say pleasantly, 'I am sure that what I have been saying has given you lots of food for thought. I will try to clarify any points about which you are unclear. What are your questions?' is more likely to guarantee a positive response.

Do not be afraid to plant a question if nobody asks one voluntarily after a short time. Once the first hurdle has been overcome, others will not feel so nervous about opening up.

Avoiding the issue will not satisfy the audience, and trying to appear to know something when you do not will not gain any admiration. If you are asked a question and you do not know the answer, it is better to admit your lack of knowledge, but try to find the answer for a later date. Bluffing can work some of the time with some people, but you must be aware of the hidden experts!

EXERCISE 3.7

Using all the ideas presented in this chapter, read through the following two extracts and make notes about tone, emphasis, pitch, etc.

Prepare the two readings and then record your presentation. Get someone else to do the same exercise and then listen to the recordings, making comments about the final result.

What lessons have you learned about your presentation skills from this activity?

Reading 1. From *The Art of War*, by Sun Tzu.

The secret of war lies in the communication. The line of supply may be said to be vital to the existence of an army as the heart to the life of a human being. Just as the duellist who finds his adversary's point menacing him with certain death, and his own guard astray, is compelled to conform to his adversary's movements, and to content himself with warding off his thrusts, so the commander whose communications are suddenly threatened finds himself in a false position, and he will be fortunate if he has not to change all his plans, to split up his force into more or less isolated detachments, and to fight with inferior numbers on ground which he has not had time to prepare, and where defeat will not be an ordinary failure, but will entail the ruin or the surrender of his whole army.

Reading 2. From *How Was It For You?*, by Maureen Lipman.

Now let's talk about oral gratification. There. That made you sit up. Thought you were reading Claire Rayner for a minute, didn't you? I'm referring, of course, to food. Throughout my memorably unmemorable life, I've often stumbled on scenes of anger and chaos whilst attempting to put fork to mouth. I don't just mean family weddings and Boxing Day lunch, either. Though where TV drama would be without such round-the-table carnage, I don't know. Take Dallas (please!). How they manage to force down so much brunch whilst thinking up so much fratricide, genocide and, no doubt, insecticide is beyond me. I reckon the ranch should be called 'Mouthfork'.

EXERCISE 3.8 GIVING THE PRESENTATION: A CHECKLIST FOR FEEDBACK TO THE PRESENTER

A. Introduction

1. Did the introduction make the subject interesting to you?

2. Did you know when the introduction had ended?

B. Voice

1. Sufficient variation of speed?

2. Sufficient variation of volume, pitch, tone?

3. Adequate pauses? Breathing OK?

C. Audience contact

1. Sufficient eye contact?

2. Would every member of the audience understand every word?

3. Any irritating mannerisms?

4. Sufficient enthusiasm shown by you for the subject?

D. Speech content

1. Correct amount of information for time allowed?

2. Did the speech follow a logical order?

3. Were the various facts well balanced?

4. Would more word pictures or analogies have helped?

E. Visual aids

1. Were any visual aids required?

2. If so, what should they have been?

F. Conclusion

1. Did you know when the conclusion had arrived?

2. Was a summary or recap required? If so, was it adequate?

3. Did the conclusion leave you with a message?

SUMMARY

By following the suggestions in this chapter you will feel more confident about making presentations, but a great deal will be learnt from practising and getting feedback from others. There is a saying that 'Experience is a great teacher', to which has been added 'the only trouble is, you get the tests before you learn the lessons!'

Before the presentation: plan and prepare.

During the presentation: speak up.

At the end: SHUT UP AND SIT DOWN!

References

Lipman, M. (1985) *How Was It For You?*, Robson Books (Futura), London.
Monkhouse, B. (1988) *Just Say a Few Words*, Lennard Publishing, London.
Moran, R. (1989) 'Tips on making speeches to international audiences', in *International Management*, Reed International, London.
Sun Tzu (1981) *The Art Of War*, Hodder and Stoughton, London.

4

Running meetings/ leading discussions

INTRODUCTION

A very well-known company which produces training films had such a success with a video entitled 'Meetings, Bloody Meetings' that it made a sequel called 'More Bloody Meetings'.

How many times have you had similar thoughts about meetings, with the belief that yet more of your precious time will be wasted sitting through a meeting which is too long, does not concern you, gets nothing done, causes ill feelings between those attending and those who have been left out, etc.?

Yet the general view about meetings, held by many organizations, is that a good meeting, properly handled, will achieve more than each participating member could have done alone and more than could be achieved by exchanging information in some other way. Meetings are not simply a communal or social alternative to memos, letters or phone calls. They can, if handled correctly, produce a dynamic effect which cannot be produced by any other means.

There are two courses of action you can follow if the feelings above are shared by you and your colleagues. You can either stop having meetings at all, or make sure that the meetings you are involved in are more efficiently and effectively run.

The first option should not be considered, but the second option means that you need to understand what meetings are all about, how a meeting should be run, and the behaviour and relationships you are likely to encounter in a meeting situation.

Types of meeting and their implications

Below are listed five types of meeting and a description of each:

1. Negotiating: to resolve some types of conflict. Discussion may be 'two-sided', and the aim will be to bring the two sides together (see Chapter 6).
2. Informing: the flow of information will tend to be only one way. Discussion is discouraged, as it may affect the passing of the information.
3. Solving problems: the creativity of the group should be used so that the problems can be solved. Structure of such a meeting will not be as precise. Discussion will flow around the table.
4. Making decisions: particular members are involved in a decision-making process. The result should be that members are informed of and committed to the decisions made. This type of meeting is fairly well structured.
5. Collecting and exchanging ideas: to present, inform and receive reactions to ideas. This type of meeting encourages discussion and questions.

EXERCISE 4.1 PURPOSES AND OBJECTIVES

1. Do you need a meeting? Is there some better/cheaper way of achieving your objectives?

2. What is the purpose of the meeting?

    (a) giving instructions?
    (b) bargaining over issues?
    (c) giving advice/counselling?
    (d) making decisions?
    (e) solving problems using others' knowledge and skills?

3. What are your overall objectives?

    (a) what do you want to achieve?
    (b) what are the best/worst results?
    (c) do you have a fallback position/contingency plans?

Perhaps the most difference similarity between these different types of meeting is the amount of control used by the chairperson to steer the events in the desired direction.

Holding a meeting is expensive in terms of time and cost. There is therefore the need to make sure that a meeting is being held for a very clear reason, that only those who need to attend do so, and that the meeting is planned effectively.

Some of the typical factors which contribute to the failure of a meeting are the following:

1. Inadequate structure: this usually occurs when there is a failure to keep the meeting to its purpose and there are one or two forceful members who dominate the proceedings.

2. Distribution and absorption of information: it may be wrongly assumed that all members will have read and understood all the information circulated prior to the meeting. Distribution of information at the meeting may wrongly assume that all in attendance can read quickly and retain every part of the information.

3. Minutes: inaccuracy of the minutes of the previous meeting leads to valuable time being taken up in the next meeting while points are reconsidered and agreed.

4. Agenda setting: if a meeting is not planned properly, the topics covered will tend to be diverse and to a certain extent time-wasting. It will also mean that some members who are not involved in certain points will lose interest in the whole proceedings.

5. Chairperson: problems associated with the chairperson are that he or she allows too much free discussion, is not clear about the purpose of the meeting or the required conclusion, and allows one or two dominant speakers to the exclusion of everyone else.

CHECKLIST 4.1   PREPARATION

1. Make action plans:
   (a) what are your sub-objectives?
   (b) do they move you forward to achieving your overall objectives?
   (c) what attitude should you adopt in the meeting? How should you approach it?

2. Prepare the structure of the meeting:
    (a) what should be the content?
    (b) what forms of process should you use?
    (c) how best to use time?
    (d) how can you set the agenda most effectively?

3. How wide are the outcomes acceptable to you?
    (a) if narrow, you want to keep the discussion closed;
    (b) if wide, you can open up the discussion.

4. How committed to the decisions do you want the participants to feel?
    (a) if high commitment is needed, involve the participants in the decision-making process;
    (b) the more control you exert, the less committed the participants will be.

The roles of chairperson and members

In a formal meeting there will be a chairperson, a recorder, and the members. To ensure a successful meeting it is important for them all to work together. All meetings have a formal and informal level because of the personal interests of all the people involved and their personal (sometimes hidden!) agendas.

Responsibilities of the chairperson

The chairperson is responsible for controlling the meeting, clarifying the objectives, handling people's contributions, ensuring a fair distribution of time to all members, ensuring that all members make a contribution and ensuring everyone knows what is expected of them following the meeting. The one thing that a chairperson should not do is to get involved with the content of the task. Responsibilities include:

- Pre-meeting

  Clarify and inform about the purpose of the meeting; set the agenda; decide on the members who are needed; decide where the meeting is to be held and the time; decide on the type of meeting to be held; circulate written material.

- During the meeting

  Set the right climate; open the meeting; control the agenda; encourage discussion; summarize; control members' contribu-

	tions; get decisions made; confirm actions and responsibilities; close the meeting.
● Post-meeting	Review the meeting; evaluate progress and results; ensure total understanding by all members.

It is important that, whatever the reason for the meeting, the right climate is created. It should be a climate of practicality of views and criticisms, and an efficient attitude towards the use of time and resources.

However, it is also important that the correct level of formality is provided for the type of group and discussion taking place. It is important that all members are put at their ease, as a relaxed climate is more likely to bring out the best in any member. Whether the meeting is held to make a decision, enforce some regulation, or announce a new project, an atmosphere that people find uncomfortable will only make them resistant, which will be counter-productive.

Positive moves should be made to set the scene for the whole meeting and thus ensure that no other person dictates the atmosphere. Some specific rules to consider are the following:

1. Begin the meeting smoothly and on time.

2. Start the meeting promptly and do not let other people's casual attitudes waste each other's time.
    Do not postpone or cancel a meeting without very good reason. By postponing or cancelling a meeting you are in fact disrupting other people's schedules. This in turn will disrupt their levels of efficiency and morale. Since the morale of staff is an all-important aspect of staff relationships, by keeping morale high you can ensure a more effective running of departments.

3. Meetings should be scheduled so that you and all the other participants have sufficient time for any necessary preparation.

4. Greet people as they arrive for the meeting and ensure that they are all seated adequately. By using a little informal conversation as they arrive you can put people at their ease. It is also important to ensure that any new member is introduced before the meeting starts.

5. As the meeting starts the topic should be set simply, clearly and early. The aim of the discussion should be set so that everyone is aware of what you want to achieve and what level of progress you would consider sufficient.

6. Help should be given to everyone to ensure that they make a contribution. The chairperson will need to recognize who is likely to act assertively, aggressively, submissively and passively. It will be necessary to compensate for any imbalance in the discussion and to do that in such a way that no-one will feel threatened or 'put down'.

7. Keep the discussion focused on one topic at a time, and avoid letting any one particular idea be developed to the detriment of others.

8. Be sure to allow only one person to speak at a time, and that only one meeting is taking place!

9. Keep the meeting moving by summarizing or recapping on the ideas which have already been presented.

10. Diffuse any tensions that may result in the meeting not reaching a satisfactory conclusion.

11. Ensure a conclusion is reached whenever possible.

EXERCISE 4.2 BEHAVIOUR AS CHAIRPERSON

Look back at the last meeting you chaired. Did you:

1. Clarify goals and objectives?

2. Set priorities?

3. Promote decision making?

4. Focus people on what they do best?

5. Bring out the best in others?

6. Were you assertive? Domineering?

7. Did you manage time well?

8. Did you communicate well with the participants? Did you ask questions? Challenge assumptions? Listen? Clarify issues? Summarize?

9. Were you aware of individuals' hidden agendas? Did you control them?

10. Did you motivate the meeting to achieve the overall objective?

What changes do you need to make in your behaviour as chairperson to become more effective?

Margerison (1974) suggests that at the beginning of a meeting it is important to ask whether anyone wishes to add an item to the agenda. This serves the purpose of allowing any member who has a 'burning' issue to make it known early, and then be able to relax in the meeting rather than sit anxiously thinking that the point will not be aired during the small amount of time designated for any other business.

Another point Margerison makes which is worth consideration is that the chairperson should discuss with the group the order in which the items should be taken, or a rationale for the priority of each item should be stated.

The chairperson needs to understand how the group functions so that he or she can be aware of the members who may need encouragement to speak and those who may need controlling.

EXAMPLE 4.1

At one regular group meeting there was an underlying conflict between two of the members. It became obvious to A that every time she spoke she would be interrupted by C. At first she thought she was imagining it all, until she sat and moved her lips as though to speak, although at this point she had nothing to say, and instantly C spoke. It became a game, as A would adopt various body movements and facial expressions which would give the illusion that she was about to speak, and C would find something to say regardless of its worth. The chairperson did not notice, and the result was a 'show-down' when A lost her temper and C accused her of never making a contribution to any of the meetings!

Responsibilities of the recorder

The recorder, often a secretary, is the person who, with the chairperson, carries out the preparation for the meeting. Detailed planning will include:

• Pre-meeting	Checks should be made on venue details, date and time; notification to attending members; necessary documents/distribution; refreshments/seating/AVA equipment.

- During the meeting   Recording of the minutes; those in attendance; actions to be taken; by whom; deadline dates.
- Post-meeting   Writing up of minutes; checking essential facts/figures; agreeing minutes with chairperson; distribution of the minutes.

Responsibilities of the members

Everyone who attends a meeting has a responsibility to make that meeting a success. It is important that all members actually understand the objective of the meeting, the agenda items and the roles of others at the meeting. Points that members should consider include:

- Pre-meeting   Research the case from a personal viewpoint; prepare a reasoned argument with supporting documents; make a note of venue, date and time details; prepare for particular role you are expected to play.
- During the meeting   Listen to the views of others; be constructive when contributing; maintain interest in item being discussed; partake in informal chairing.
- Post-meeting   Complete any tasks allocated at the meeting.

It is important that everyone is prepared to put forward constructive ideas and to decide on the best solution for the problem being presented, even if it means modifying or surrendering your own views.

If a meeting covers several different areas, it is possible that interest could be lost by members once their particular area of expertise has been dealt with. The level of interest should be maintained as much as possible as it is often found that good ideas are forthcoming from a combination of abilities.

If a chairperson fails to fulfil his/her function in a proper fashion one of the members should raise the point of order in a tactful manner. The worst possible situation would be one in which a chairperson loses complete control of a meeting and it would be up to a member to regain some sort of control. It would be necessary to help the chairperson in as diplomatic a manner as possible to avoid any conflict.

EXERCISE 4.3

Study the meetings highlighted below and describe what you need to take into consideration to make them as effective as possible. Think in terms of the following points:

- Where should the meeting take place?
- What should the seating and room arrangements be?
- The timing involved: how much notice should be given and what time of day chosen?
- What sort of information would you expect the members to have prior knowledge of, and to bring to the meeting?

The meetings

1. A newly formed group meets each week to discuss the priorities for the forthcoming week.

2. A new policy is being introduced throughout the organization and the meeting is with your subordinates to inform and discuss reactions to the policy.

3. A meeting is arranged where you are to represent the thoughts of all department heads in your section. The meeting to consider is the one you must have with your colleagues prior to the full meeting.

Behaviour in meetings

There are three types of behaviour in meetings:

1. Task behaviour
2. Maintenance behaviour
3. Self-directed behaviour (hidden agendas)

Task behaviour moves the meeting towards achievement of the objectives, towards achieving a high-quality outcome within time constraints. Such behaviour includes:

- Analyzing the information available.
- Identifying knowledge resources.

- Defining the problems.
- Making proposals.
- Establishing criteria for success.
- Determining solutions.
- Agreeing the best solution.
- Planning presentation.
- Evaluating.
- Summarizing.

It also includes the procedures to be followed:

- Whether to appoint a chairperson/secretary.
- How to allocate preparatory work.
- What rules to apply.
- When and how to record ideas.
- When to review procedures.

Maintenance behaviour employs social skills to address the issues of how people feel as participants in the meeting and to maintain social harmony:

- How to handle the meeting.
- Who influences whom.
- Who talks to whom, how often, and why.
- Who contributes and who does not, and why.
- Getting genuine commitment.
- Supporting each other's proposals.
- Gatekeeping.
- Encouraging.
- Harmonizing/reducing tension.
- Giving feedback.

Self-directed behaviour occurs when people are trying to achieve their own personal objectives in the meeting, which may or may not be congruent with the overall objective for which the meeting was convened (hidden agendas). Some examples are the following:

- Attacking/defending your own/others' positions.
- Blocking each other's proposals/being negative/stating difficulties without reasoned argument.
- Diverting the discussion away from areas where you feel threatened or weak.
- Seeking sympathy: making others feel sorry for you and therefore willing to support you.
- Looking for recognition for the value of your contributions.
- Withdrawing: refusing to make a contribution.
- Point scoring: trying to score points off others to enhance your status.
- Monopolizing the discussion.
- Horsing around: trivializing others' contributions.

The main reasons for this kind of behaviour are:

- Difficulties in identifying with the group.
- Problems of conflicting goals and needs.
- A need for recognition.
- Problems of power and influence.

If the existence of these self-oriented behaviour patterns can be recognized and the causes understood, there is a greater chance that undercurrents may diminish, leading to increased effectiveness in task and maintenance processes.

Use the grid in Checklist 4.2 to record your behaviour as a chairperson. Ask a participant or an observer to: (a) recognize the different types of behaviour you exhibit and record them in the appropriate boxes; and (b) to tick each type of behaviour as it occurs, and try to record short quotes showing examples from the meeting which characterize that behaviour.

CHECKLIST 4.2   PERFORMANCE AS CHAIRPERSON

Behaviour	Frequency (tick)	Quotes/examples
Structuring the meeting		
Setting reviewing targets		
Timekeeping		
Encouraging ideas, suggestions, problems		
Clarifying		
Testing understanding, consensus		
Bringing in/shutting out		
Building commitment to decisions		
Premature closure/unclear outcomes		
Adding pace, impetus/slowing down		
Over-control/under-control		
Dealing with conflict		
Reviewing progress/summarizing		
Closing the meeting		

The chairperson has the heavy responsibility to integrate these types of behaviour to make the meeting work, especially so that self-directed behaviour will not be disruptive and time-wasting.

All the skills dealt with in Chapter 3 (Making Presentations) are relevant to the context of meetings. This applies even though meetings are essentially interactive events with equal contributions from all the members. To ensure that you can effectively participate in meetings you should consider the following aspects:

- You are well prepared.
- Speech is clear and persuasive.
- Criticism is constructive.
- Questioning is clear and constructive.
- Behaviour exhibited is confident and assertive (but not aggressive).

Being well prepared means dealing with the logistics, paperwork, research and contributions needed for a meeting. A checklist is given at the end of the chapter which highlights the questions you need to ask yourself in each of these areas.

Being clear and persuasive indicates that, in any meeting where you are called upon to make a contribution, you will be concise, interesting and confident. In many organizations things are often said and decided in private after the meeting. In some they are never said nor agreed at all, mainly because people feel that their contribution will not be given enough serious thought (see Chapter 3 on Making Presentations).

Constructive criticism will alert people to the fact that you are listening to them. This will encourage them to listen to you. You should listen carefully and with tolerance, making notes where appropriate. Some points worth considering are:

1. Summarizing what the last speaker has said will show your understanding and provide a platform for you to make your point.

2. Do not enter into a debate unless you have a valid contribution to make, as this tends to take up too much time and often detracts from the question in hand.

3. Do not accept an interruption unless it is allowed by the chair-person. Be polite and assertive and continue with what you have to say.

4. Only criticize constructively, even if some ideas are very obviously of little use or interest.

5. Agreeing with something simply to conform with the majority is not a good idea. Once you have looked carefully at your reasons for disagreeing and wish to maintain your ideas, you should state your objections and have them recorded.

6. Disagreeing with something even though your argument has been

proved to have little basis is also of little use. Have the grace to admit that the argument against your idea is sound.

Questions should be clear and constructive so that all the implications of views expressed can be clearly understood. Do not worry about your need to ask questions to clarify points or even to ask for a summary of the views expressed. Make sure that your questions are to the point, that they have a constructive purpose and that they are put in a way which will not cause embarrassment to yourself or to the person being addressed. Instead of saying, 'Hang on, I don't understand that!', 'That really doesn't make any sense at all', or 'This is ridiculous, you've lost me', it would be better to say, 'Could you recap on that last point?', 'Correct me if I am wrong but are you saying . . .?' and 'Could we have a summary of the position so far?'

Your behaviour should be one of professionalism, confidence and assertiveness. Once you are clear about the way meetings should be handled and your own part in a meeting, then your behaviour will be more positive, rational and assertive, allowing you to put your points across in an effective way and without infringing upon the rights of the other members present. Within the context of a meeting your behaviour should be expressed by clear questioning, a confident voice and manner, eye contact with other participants and a tolerant approach to questions/interruptions.

Relationships within groups, teams and meetings

To ensure that any meeting is held in a constructive and purposeful manner it is important that the following are taken into account:

1. The aim of the meeting should be to progress through a combination of ideas presented by people with differing interests and skills.
2. The group of people involved should be aware of the aims and objectives of the meeting and should work towards that, rather than for their own personal points of view.
3. The climate should be one in which all ideas are listened to and encouraged, with criticism being positive and constructive.

To be able to put these ideas into practice it is important to understand something about group dynamics, group development and group behaviour.

Group dynamism comes from the ability to accept and share various ideas, to criticize from all aspects, to encourage and stimulate the imagination, to reject ill-suited ideas fairly quickly and to recognize possible solutions early. Such dynamism has to be worked for and needs a tolerant and assertive attitude from all the members. The greatest enemies of an effective meeting are probably best described as bureaucracy, intolerance and the inefficient use of time.

Within any organization, groups usually fall into four categories:

- formal groups
- informal groups
- primary groups
- secondary groups

In the context of the organization, the main groups to which individuals belong are their work groups, created by design (Formal Groups). They may also form relationships with sets of others with similar interests (Informal Groups), which evolve to satisfy the needs of the members. Secondary groups are relatively large groups, the size of which constrains the personal interactions which can take place between all the members (e.g. the US Senate, a football crowd). Primary groups are those in which members have frequent personal contact and are working in a common task e.g. the work groups, the family, a small social group, and which are major influences on the individuals' values and attitudes. In most organizations, the work group can be described as a Formal Primary Group.

The needs of the individuals within the groups are described by Maslow (1971) as a hierarchy composed of:

- survival needs (hunger, thirst . . .)
- security and safety needs (protection against threats . . .)
- social needs (friendship . . .)
- self-esteem needs (status, recognition . . .)
- self-actualization needs (achieving your full potential . . .)

Kakabadse, Ludlow and Vinnicombe (1987) identify another need as the need for personal power. This can be satisfied within a group either as power over the other members of the group, or by using the power of the whole group as a lever to effect changes in the organization.

George Homans (1951) established that all groups have three elements in common:

1. *Activities:* what people do in groups. Some activities are completed to satisfy personal needs, others to achieve the group task and some to achieve harmony within the group. They may be prescribed by the organization or carried out by individual choice.

2. *Sentiments:* values, beliefs and attitudes which individuals take with them to a group situation. The social power of the group is great in the sense that new members can be socialized into attitudes and behaviour that they did not possess or had not clarified before entry. It is important from the organization's point of view that the new behaviour fits in with what is required.

3. *Interaction:* interpersonal transactions occur between group members. The behaviour displayed is relevant to both task achievement and maintenance of group harmony and morale and to achieving the satisfaction of personal needs.

Apart from the fact that these three elements are evident within groups, Homans also established that groups showed 'required' behaviour and 'emergent' behaviour.

Required behaviour is what the organization sees as necessary for task performance and membership of the organization. Members are informed of this and are rewarded for fulfilling the requirements. The behaviour required can take many forms but is often seen in such behaviour as punctuality, co-operation with other members of the organization, and achievement of performance standards.

Emergent behaviour is what the individual members actually do, either within the organization's principles or as a modification of them. Individuals make individual decisions on emergent behaviour.

It is the processes that the group uses and the roles that the individual members adopt which influence the success of the group. In the context of meetings, this means the way the meeting runs, and the roles people choose to play in the meeting itself. Understanding the type of group the meeting members are likely to comprise, the levels of needs of the individuals participating, the tasks to be completed, the sentiments they bring with them, and the likely ways in which they will interact with each other, the roles they prefer to play, will enable you to plan your most appropriate strategy for your personal participation in the meeting.

The roles we play in group situations

Belbin (1981) examined the behaviour of various groups working on a management game. Using psychometric measures to analyze the people who made up the successful teams, he established that such teams were made up of people who could work in eight different roles. When these eight roles were truly represented, the groups appeared to be well balanced and to work in a more flexible and resourceful manner. The eight roles represented the following characters:

1. *The chairperson:* he/she clarifies group objectives and sets the agenda. Guiding, co-ordinating, communicating are the main functions.

2. *The shaper:* the task leader who gives shape to the group, unites ideas and produces some sort of pattern.

3. *The plant:* the 'ideas' person who looks for innovative approaches to a problem, although there is a tendency to dismiss the importance of detail.

4. *The monitor/evaluator:* regarded as the analyst, and good at assimilating, interpreting and evaluating data.

5. *The company worker:* the practical organizer of the group, turning ideas into manageable tasks.

6. *The resource investigator:* he/she helps maintain morale and enthusiasm and has an excellent network making him/her a 'Mr Fix-it'.

7. *The team worker:* aware of individual needs and worries, he/she manages conflict and smooths out difficulties. An essential person when the group is experiencing difficulties.

8. *The finisher:* also known as the progress chaser, he/she works to a deadline and tends to demand an orderly way of working.

Belbin points out that although people show characteristics of all of these roles, they do tend to have some long-term stability of role preference. He continues by stating that although preferences do not change much over time, participation in roles which are compatible to their main role often develops. Try to identify what your preferred role is and those of your work group – it will assist your team development.

Handling conflict

One of the most necessary skills to possess for holding effective meetings is the ability to handle conflict. How many times have you been in a meeting when tensions, conflicts and difficulties between individual members have caused a major block to the implementation of ideas and the finding of a positive solution to a problem?

Conflict can arise because of a disagreement about a particular point or even because of the manner in which discussions have taken place. To ensure that there is a greater amount of collaboration and commitment in meetings, the following points should be considered:

1. *Active listening:* this involves paying close attention to what the person speaking is saying and doing. Communication is through words, emotions and body language. The words reflect the intellectual side of the message, the feelings reflect the emotions involved concerning the subject in question, and the body language gives a negative or positive response. A speaker should be given the chance to verbalize his or her thoughts with a minimum of interruption and the maximum amount of help from open questions, probe questions, clarification of ideas and head nodding.

2. *Assertiveness:* being assertive will give a positive reaction to any conflict and, if you are in the chairperson's position, will maintain control over the meeting. Showing assertive behaviour is, according to Back and Back (1987): 'standing up for your own rights in such a way that you do not violate another person's rights' and 'expressing your needs, wants, opinions, feelings and beliefs in direct, honest and appropriate ways'.

3. *Reducing communication blocks:* this must be achieved by reducing any threatening, dominating or aggressive behaviour. It is also important to encourage those who find it difficult to voice their opinions because of the more dominant personalities present.

4. *Emphasis of issues:* issues should be voiced and all the necessary facts gathered. Large issues should be broken down into smaller, manageable ones and problems should be dealt with one at a time. Most importantly – emphasize issues, not personalities!

5. *Decision on actions to be taken:* appraisal of actions and their possible

consequences should be made, and the agreement of all members obtained concerning the course of any action which needs to be taken. This will act as a deterrent to any conflict at future meetings when the results have to be discussed.

The final word goes to Charles Margerison (1974) who says: 'What is absolutely necessary is the skill to talk to others in groups, to resolve problems, and to seek opportunities. This demands high interpersonal communication skills . . .'

CHECKLIST 4.3   PREPARATION FOR A MEETING

The Domestic Arrangements	• Venue, time, length of meeting
	• Who should attend
	• Who will chair
	• Who will be called upon to speak
Paperwork	• The agenda
	• Minutes from previous meeting
	• Reports to be read beforehand
	• Written reports or graphics wanted at the meeting
Purpose/preparation	• What do you want to achieve?
	• What kind of meeting is it?
	• Do you need to canvass for views?
	• Do you need to acquire specialist advice on any subject?
	• Are you conversant with the reason for the meeting?
	• Do you need to discuss any of the content of the meeting with anyone in a higher management position?
Contributions	• Do you need to use visual aids?
	• Is a written report going to be needed?
	• How much general knowledge of the subject is there?
	• If you have a presentation to make, have you read through the necessary points to consider and followed them?

EXERCISE 4.4 SELECTION COMMITTEE

This is an exercise to give practice in meeting skills. The use of a video recorder is essential. Apart from the people participating in the mock meeting, there should be one or two people as observers. It is envisaged that there are at least four people participating in the meeting. It is interesting to have three or four groups working on this exercise at the same time, especially when it comes to the decisions made concerning who is to be promoted.

Each participant is asked to present a case for a person, from within his or her department, who is being considered for promotion within the organization. Each participant should consider him/herself to be in a middle management position, and to be given a different candidate description, which has been written to take into account the organization's requirements for post holders. The description is of the person each participant has selected for promotion from his/her department. It is assumed that he or she is very aware of the candidate's abilities to meet the job requirements. The description is to be studied and the information prepared for presentation at the meeting.

The discussion is within the group, and you have 45 minutes to discuss the candidates and to make a decision about which one should be promoted. The candidates are to be ranked from one down because of the possibility of further vacancies arising.

The observers can have the use of a tally sheet to direct them to particular types of behaviour, but it is their job to observe the meeting and to report back at the end of the exercise. Questions the observers should consider:

- Who made the most/least effective contribution?
- How clear was the purpose of the meeting?
- How well did people listen?
- What were the most helpful actions?
- Was the time well used?
- Were difficult issues dealt with well?
- Did the group distinguish between fact and opinion?
- What type of questions were used to establish facts and views?
- How were decisions made?

SUMMARY

In this chapter we have examined the various types of meeting we are likely to encounter at work, and how to manage them. Remember that any meeting is likely to cover several issues and topics – a meeting that started out as a vehicle for solving problems may move into a negotiating one as more information is contributed, and so on. So you need to vary your style of chairing to meet the needs of the situation. Be organized and use your skills, and meetings will turn out to be successful.

References

Back, Ken and Back, Kate (1987) *Assertiveness at Work: A practical guide to handling awkward situations*, Guild Publishing, London.

Belbin, R. M. (1981) *Management Teams: Why they succeed or fail*, Heinemann, London.

Buchanan, D. and Huczynski, A. (1985) *Organisational Behaviour*, Prentice Hall International, Hemel Hempstead.

Homans, G. (1951) *The Human Group*, Routledge and Kegan Paul, London.

Kakabadse, A., Ludlow, R. and Vinnicombe, S. (1987) *Working in Organisations*, Gower, London.

Margerison, C. (1974) *Managerial Problem Solving*, McGraw-Hill, Maidenhead.

Maslow, A. H. (1971) *Motivation and Personality*, Harper and Row, New York.

5

Conducting surveys

INTRODUCTION

Organizations often realize that they face problems, but need extra information to solve them. Problems of performance, employee relations, labour turnover, need a clear understanding of the way employees see their working environment before solutions can be found.

Communication upwards can become a major problem in most organizations. People are often hesitant to speak about their work and their jobs – they do not want to stick their necks out – and even if they do, there's no guarantee that the information will reach top management. This means that decisions are frequently made which affect the organization and its workforce with little or no knowledge of how the employees feel about them.

As it has become increasingly obvious that employees are demanding much more from work than a pay packet at the end of the week, as they want increasingly to be involved in decision making on matters which affect them, organizations spend a great deal of time and money to identify their employees' attitudes and feelings. Suggestion boxes, employee committees, quality teams have been used to gather this information. In many cases it has been inadequate. Anonymity cannot be guaranteed, it is difficult to probe areas of motivation and morale, and often the information is not properly analyzed and incorrect interpretations are made.

One of the best means of acquiring the relevant, valid information you need is to take a survey approach. Much of the data which is used by social scientists is obtained by means of a survey. There are many different kinds of surveys, from censuses to opinion polls, to market research studies, to attitude studies.

Surveys may also vary in their objectives, their extent and the time and money available to fund them, but they are generally designed to collect a large quantity of information of different kinds.

There are three main reasons for implementing surveys. Surveys are often conducted in order to **describe** a population, i.e. the information is used to elaborate on the attributes of the population. In some cases there may be an element of **explanation,** e.g. where the information obtained is used to clarify relationships within the population. Surveys can also be used in the initial stages of research as a **search** or **exploratory** device used to elicit further information about the population.

Sampling

In most cases it is not feasible to study the entire population under consideration. For example, it would be very time-consuming and costly to survey all individuals in a very large company. Therefore, surveys usually look at a smaller section of the whole population – a **sample**. A sampling frame is the complete list from which a sample is taken and individuals are selected from within this frame of reference. The object of taking a sample is to choose a group of people who are typical of the population so that the results of the sample can be considered as representative of the results for the total population. In choosing a sample, it is important to obtain as true a representation of the total population as possible.

Sampling theory has three main sections: the **selection process**, the **estimation process** and the **inference process**.

The **selection process** states the rules used to select the members of the sample. There are a number of ways in which the sample can be selected to try to eliminate bias and achieve representativeness. Some of the basic processes are outlined below.

Simple random sampling involves the selection of individuals on a totally arbitrary basis. In this case, the probability of being chosen as a member of the sample is no greater for one individual than for another, therefore there is no bias in who is selected as part of the sample.

In some cases simple random sampling may not be the most appropriate method to use. This may be because it is not possible to obtain a random sample or because it may not be the best method to achieve a representative sample. **Systematic sampling** methods can then be an alternative. In systematic sampling the sampling frame is set and every ninth element is chosen for inclusion in the sample.

Stratified sampling is a modification of the random sampling approach. Stratified sampling is used to increase the degree of representativeness of the sample. In this case, rather than selecting from the total sampling frame, the appropriate numbers of individuals are drawn from homogeneous subsets of the population. For example, the total population in an organization can be said to consist of a number of groups of individuals: board of directors, senior managers, middle managers, supervisors, work force. This is a very simple grouping. In stratified sampling representative numbers from each of these groupings would be chosen for the sample.

On some occasions it may be appropriate to select the sample on the basis of previous knowledge of the population. In this case, **quota sampling** can be used. This is a method which involves classifying the individuals in the population into groupings, e.g. by sex/age/management level. All individuals are assigned a weighting according to their proportion of the total population and the sample drawn from these subgroups of individuals.

The estimation and inference processes

Various statistical methods are used in the processes of estimation and inference where the results obtained from the sample are used as estimates of the results for the total population and to make generalizations.

Types of survey designs and variables

There are several different survey designs available. Two of the more common are **cross-sectional** surveys and **longitudinal** surveys. Cross-sectional surveys gather information from a large number of people at one point in time, e.g. a Gallup poll. Longitudinal surveys allow the collection of data over a period of time at different points and can be useful in showing changes over time. There are two broad distinctions in the types of variables obtainable in surveys. Some variables are qualitative in nature, e.g. a person's occupation or the management style of a company. Quantitative variables are those which give a measure of magnitude, such as an individual's income or the annual turnover of a firm. For a more detailed review of the principles of sampling design refer to Babbie (1973).

Planning

A survey has two main parts. One part consists of the design of the survey and collection of the data. The second part involves the analysis of the data. In planning a survey, the whole process needs to be considered at the outset, as the initial design stage determines what can be done at later stages. Basically the end products (whether these are reports, discussions, statistical results, or recommendations) determine all of the preceding stages.

The planning process should include the drafting of an appropriate timetable for the project, and the setting of a realistic time scale. Issues such as the overall logistics of the project, access to the population sample, the data collection process, type of analysis required and the format of the results need careful consideration at the outset.

A well-structured and -organized survey can produce information on employee opinions and can help management to:

- Identify and analyze attitudes towards the company, its policies and practices.
- Measure levels of morale and motivation.
- Identify specific problems in departments and sections.

It also gives employees the opportunity to:

- Get things off their chest.
- Give their opinions on aspects of the organization (anonymously).
- Make suggestions for improvement.
- Become aware of possible change.

Objectives

Before starting on the survey process, you must identify what your objectives are: is there a problem and can a survey give you the information you require to solve it? You have then to consider the urgency and importance of the problem and the political implications of conducting a survey (feelings, unions, etc.), and to weigh the costs against the possible benefits; and paramount in your considerations must be that, if you do collect the information, will any action be taken on it?

Success in the process depends on careful planning and co-operation from all parties involved. You are more likely to achieve success if you agree objectives, methods to be used, administration, and the way in which these will be communicated to staff at all levels of management, with union representations and staff representatives. If you try just to impose the operation without consultation, you are doomed to failure. You need to gain their commitment first before proceeding.

The planning stage must also include the means of collating and analyzing data, feedback mechanisms, publication of results and recommended actions; and what questions are to be asked, and how, and from whom. If you have time, the question design and methods used can be checked and modified through a pilot study with a small representative sample.

Methods of collecting data

In the majority of surveys, data is obtained by asking people questions. Questions may be asked by interviewers in face-to-face interviews, over the telephone, or in a written form in questionnaires. The questions are usually drawn up in some form of questionnaire schedule which is used to direct the interview or to ask the respondent about specific issues. This can either be in a semi-structured format, often used in face-to-face interviews, or in the structured format of a questionnaire.

Using questionnaires

Questions must be designed to obtain the information which you seek, and the replies must be comparable. They need therefore to be specific, and couched in clear, unambiguous language. To classify the responses, demographic information is needed, e.g. age, sex, length of service, department, while still retaining the anonymity of the responder.

Designing questions is not as simple as it might appear. Check carefully with others, especially psychometricians if possible, and try to conduct a pilot survey to ensure you have your wording right. Many 'don't know' responses indicate your questions may be worded vaguely; clusters of answers at extremes may indicate leading questions and bias your interpretation.

Consider also the order of your questions: do not start off with a sequence of complex questions which require lengthy thought – you will lose the interest of the responder and it is probable that later questions will be answered perfunctorily. Vary the complexity of your questions in your sequence and ask a similar question in different words in a different context to reinforce the responses you are getting.

You can use three basic types of question to gain the information you require:

1. Closed questions
2. Open questions
3. Rating/ranked questions

Closed questions require a closed answer: there is choice only for the respondent, e.g.: sex? male or female? 'Were you at work last Friday?' Yes or No.

Open questions allow for discussion by the respondent on the content of the question, e.g.: 'What effect is the recent introduction of word-processors having on your work performance?' enables a secretary to amplify and discuss her thoughts and attitudes on this change.

Rating/ranked questions allow the respondent to classify his or her response by rating on a defined scale or to rank his/her response in a series of categories. They are lists of statements which have to be ticked in response, as illustrated here:

Statement	*Response*
This is the worst organization I have ever worked for	Agree/Don't know/Disagree

or

Statement	*Factors*
Rank these three factors in order of importance to you at work (1 = most important, 3 = least important)	• A good salary • Good relationship with boss • A challenging job

Closed questions give you information which is easy to analyze, but your questions may not be designed to dig deeper than the symptoms of a problem. Open questions give you a lot of information which you may find difficult to interpret if you are not expert in content analysis. Rating/ranking questions give you information which can be analyzed in a quantifiable way – you are getting a measure of the actual position on the attitude continuum of the person's feelings. But again, their effectiveness boils down to good choice of questions and good choice of scales.

A great deal of research has been done on the design of questions and questionnaires. The way in which questions are presented has been shown to affect the quality of the responses. You need to ensure that the right questions are asked, in the right way, and are understood by the respondent. A poorly disguised questionnaire, or inappropriate presentation of the questions will tend to increase the amount of non-response in a survey.

CHECKLIST 5.1   DESIGNING QUESTIONNAIRES

Objectives

1.   Are you clear about your objective for using a questionnaire?
2.   What information do you want to obtain?
3.   What are you going to do with it when you have it?
4.   What are you trying to achieve, specifically, in measurable terms?
5.   Can the information really be found with a questionnaire?
6.   Would it be better to use available data and follow up with a call or something else?

Qualitative surveys

If your objective is to measure the views of a small group, consider the following:

1.   Questions can be open-ended, asking for opinions – but questions must not be too general (people just won't bother to answer them).
2.   The best approach may be to use a multiple-choice approach to possible answers, giving clues to the type of response required with some room for other answers.
3.   Decide how you are going to analyze responses before designing the questionnaire. Handraulic? Computerized database?

Quantitative Surveys

For larger surveys, which must be analyzed in a more concrete way:

1. Questions need to be close-ended.
2. Techniques you can use include:
   (a) attitude scaling (how much, on a scale of 1–7, do you agree with . . .?).
   (b) multiple-choice questions: initial research / pilot study / telephone calls / visits / desk research may be needed before multiple-choice questions can be developed.

General points

1. Remember to ask for the name and address of the responder on the form, unless anonymity is required.
2. Ask the straightforward and least controversial questions first.
3. Keep the questionnaire as short as possible.
4. The covering letter should be short and make clear the objectives.
5. Use dotted lines for respondents to write on.
6. Group your questions under sub-headings, to make it easier for the respondent.
7. Put boxes on right or left of options as it makes it easier to see which box refers to each question, and be consistent.
8. Questions should be clear, not ambiguous.
9. Each question should not deal with more than one issue.
10. A good layout will encourage people to bother to reply.

Using interviews

A survey interview is simply a conversation whereby the interviewer obtains certain information from the respondent. Interviews can be unstructured, where the topic is discussed very generally. This is often used as an exploratory exercise to find out the scope and extent of data about the topic. Semi-structured interviews involve a more directive approach from the interviewer. There may be a number of specific areas that the interview must cover but scope is allowed for the interviewer to elaborate opinions, feelings and ideas. Structured interviews involve asking well-defined, pre-set questions, usually in a formal questionnaire format.

Specifically, the use of interviews will only be effective if:

1. The interviewee has access to the necessary information.

2. The questions are framed in such a manner that he/she understands what information is required, e.g.: 'What do you think of the Norfolk broads?' has different connotations to an Englishman and an American.

3. The interviewer must ensure that the respondent understands his role in the situation and the manner in which he/she should respond. This can be taught by means of probe questions which investigate further to elicit the information required.

4. The respondent must want to co-operate to answer accurately. He/she has co-operated so far by agreeing to be interviewed – and the interviewer is responsible for ensuring this motivation is maintained by establishing a rapport between them.

CHECKLIST 5.2   INTERVIEWS

1. Objective of the interview: are you clear about this? Is the respondent clear? Is an interview the best way to get the information you need?

2. Setting: the environment in which the interview is conducted influences greatly its success or failure. Choose a setting which is non-threatening to the interviewee, and keep free from interruptions and distractions.

3. Length: the interviewee should be told beforehand how long the interview will take. Stick rigidly to this: do not overrun – remember he/she has a schedule to keep to as well as you. The scheduled length of the interview should be as long as you estimate you need to collect the information and no longer.

4. Interview skills: use the interview skills discussed in Chapter 2.

5. Preparation: prepare as for any interview – structure and control by the use of questions; establish rapport quickly at the beginning; maintain the motivation of the respondent throughout.

6. Recording: record the information received by the use of notes/checklists against your prepared list of questions. In an unstructured or semi-structured interview the use of a tape recorder can speed up the process and enable the interviewer to listen more accurately and so identify more clearly where probe questions are necessary for clarification. People may be nervous initially about being recorded, but they quickly forget the recorder is there. But remember to switch it on!

Self-completion questionnaire

Face-to-face or telephone interviews are time-consuming and expensive to execute, so if the sample is large, or it is important to obtain the information quickly, a self-completion questionnaire is often used. It is potentially more confidential than interviews and is widely used in survey research. There are a number of issues to consider when using the self-completion questionnaire.

Introduction and briefing
A typical self-completion questionnaire is handed to the respondents. They must be motivated to provide the relevant information, and an introduction and briefing is one of the first steps in generating this motivation. This introduction should be brief and to the point. It should outline the purpose of the survey and provide information about what will be done with the results. Sample 5.1 provides an illustration.

Length of the questionnaire
The length of the questionnaire is another important consideration. A very lengthy questionnaire may provoke the potential respondent to assign it to the nearest bin. On the other hand, a very brief questionnaire that excludes important questions is a waste of time and effort. It is therefore important to try to achieve a balance between the length of the questionnaire and the relevance of the questions asked. These considerations will ultimately influence the total length of the questionnaire.

Layout of the questionnaire
The layout of the questionnaire makes an immediate impression on respondents and can also be very important in encouraging or discouraging them to complete the questionnaire. The layout should convey an impression of simplicity and ease of completion. Questions should not look cramped and difficult to read. The use of subsections for similar types of question helps to simplify the questionnaire. Enough space should be allowed for answers to open-ended questions. It is often better to start with the easier, factual questions, reserving more difficult questions for later, when the respondent has been committed to completing the questionnaire.

Style
Adequate, simple and explicit instructions should be given as to how to complete the questionnaire, such as, 'tick only one box', or 'write an

Sample 5.1   Covering letter for a questionnaire

TO ALL STAFF

Date

The company would like to collect information about the way employees think and feel about their jobs. All members of staff are requested to complete the attached attitude survey form, and I should like to ask you personally for your co-operation. The exercise will only be of real value if we get considered, honest and truthful answers from a large majority of staff.

Your answers will be entirely confidential. At no time will anyone attempt to find out what was said by any individual.

The purpose of the survey is to collect information. The company will consider seriously all the issues raised by the survey, and everyone will be informed of the results when they have been collated and analyzed.

Thank you for helping us to address these issues.

Managing Director

---

answer in the space provided'. A consistent style for the questions should be adopted throughout: if the questionnaire begins by asking respondents to tick boxes then, if possible, do not switch to circling numbers in later questions.

Badly worded or badly constructed questions can not only lead the respondent to non-response, but can push a respondent to a biased answer in a particular question, or create confusion as to what the question is asking: therefore it is important to try to avoid bias in questions. Sample 5.2 suggests a layout of questions and instructions for your questionnaire.

Anonymity and confidentiality

The use of questionnaires for gathering data has potential consequences for the respondents, particularly if the information is of a sensitive nature. Some respondents will welcome the opportunity to

Sample 5.2   Sample questions and instructions

Section 2

Please read each statement and decide how you feel about it. You may be undecided about some. To help you express your opinion, five possible answers are given beside the question as in this example:

	Strongly agree	Agree	Neither agree nor disagree	Disagree	Strongly disagree
I am very satisfied with my job	1	2	3	4	5

Just choose the answer which most closely reflects your opinion and circle the number under it. Some of the statements may not be worded exactly the way you would like them, but try to interpret them the best way you can.

Be sure to mark every statement. Circle only one answer for each statement. Please do not skip any statements.

Question 4

In your job do you tend to agree or disagree with the following statements?

	Strongly agree	Agree	Neither agree nor disagree	Disagree	Strongly disagree
(a) Your working conditions are good.	1	2	3	4	5
(b) You are well paid.	1	2	3	4	5
(c) Your work is interesting.	1	2	3	4	5
(d) Management cares about you as a person.	1	2	3	4	5
(e) You get recognition for a job well done.	1	2	3	4	5

	Strongly agree	Agree	Neither agree nor disagree	Disagree	Strongly disagree
(f) There are good opportunities for promotion.	1	2	3	4	5
(g) You are able to use your initiative.	1	2	3	4	5
(h) Your colleagues are very helpful when you have a problem.	1	2	3	4	5

voice their opinion, but many may be reluctant to do this if the information can be traced back to them. Therefore, it is often advisable to use questionnaires which are anonymous and which do not ask respondents to identify themselves in any way. It is useful to give an assurance that the information will not be used in a way that will identify individuals or that results will only be published in aggregate form. Although this approach makes it impossible to follow up with respondents and ask further questions or clarify comments, it may be worth sacrificing this opportunity to achieve more honest and open responses. Potential insights may only be attainable through this approach. Sample 5.3 sets out a survey introduction to be sent to respondents.

Non-response
As surveys usually aim to achieve a representative view of the total population via the selected sample, it is important that every member of the sample be polled. Non-response is undesirable as it decreases the number of viable responses from the sample and thus calls into question the representativeness of the results.

Analyzing the data

Processing the results

When the questionnaires have been returned and/or the interviews conducted, it is necessary to reduce the mass of data they contain to

Sample 5.3   A survey introduction to be sent to respondents

The objective of this survey is to find out more about how people feel and think about their jobs. The information provided will be used to aid decisions on management and personnel policies. We need to know more about what people feel about their jobs in order to develop and implement better solutions to problems.

All your individual suggestions and comments will count. We are anxious to have your own personal views and ideas. If you prefer not to complete the survey at the office, take it home with you. If you have any queries, do not hesitate to get in touch with me.

The survey

The survey is confidential and anonymous. You are not asked to sign your name. Your answers will be coded and processed together with the answers of all the other respondents and the final report will reveal only what groups of people have answered. No attempt will be made to identify any individual respondent.

You are being given the form in an envelope with your name on it, but we do not want you to sign it or return it in the same envelope. On the first page of the questionnaire we have written personal coded information on your department, age, sex and grade. This information is included on the form to enable us to establish if there are differing responses from different sections. Because of this coding it is important that you fill in and return the actual form given to you in the return self-addressed envelope attached.

The information on each completed questionnaire will be analyzed by computer to show the findings for all the staff, and the differences in responses between staff of different age, sex, and grade. A report of these findings will be made available to everyone as soon as the data has been processed, analyzed, and written up.

In order to make absolutely certain that the final analysis is completely anonymous, no calculations will normally be made for groups of less than ten people.

Your co-operation in giving us some of your time to complete this questionnaire is much appreciated.

useful, manageable information upon which decisions can be made. This is a process which involves a considerable amount of 'number crunching'. Coding is the process of allocating codes/shorthand symbols to the collected data. The main purpose of coding is to facilitate analysis of the data collected and by implication to summarize the data. The actual choice of codes depends on the equipment used (sometimes your own head, sometimes by calculator, increasingly by computer) to analyze the data, and sometimes on the analysis itself. Therefore, if data is to be analyzed by computer, codes are restricted to the set of characters the computer can read, usually alphabetic or numerical. Coding cannot take place until after the data collection, but needs to be considered at the design stage of the survey and in particular at the time of designing the questionnaire: for example, space needs to be left on the questionnaire for the coding.

The data analysis does not necessarily have to be statistical. Qualitative data (e.g. opinions, feelings) are difficult to analyze in this way, but it is more usual to use statistical methods based on quantitative data, backed up by relevant use of the qualitative data, to give a general and specific 'feel' of the findings for presentation.

Analysis by computer

The design, execution and analysis of the survey should not be considered as separate issues but as an integrated whole, with the earlier stages taking account of the method of final analysis. There are several standard computer packages for statistical analysis, and in particular for survey analysis. These are widely available but you need to check which packages are available on computer and whether there are any restrictions in operation. The manuals of the programs contain details of the forms of input of data, size of data set, options available and the commands to use.

Interpreting data

When the operations of preparation of data for the computer (coding/ data input) and the detection and correction of errors have been completed there is the possibility of using the computer to generate new variables from the input data. The results of the analysis then require careful consideration and interpretation.

It is important to look beyond the analysis of the data to how the results will be used, and how they will be written up and communicated. Your task in this stage of the survey is not just to present the results in a logical, convenient form and leave the reader to draw his own conclusions, but also to include your own ideas based on the results obtained.

Feedback

Feedback on the results is particularly important in the case of surveying in organizations. The promise of feedback can be used as an additional incentive to the respondents to complete and return the questionnaire. Feedback on the results of the survey can also be used as a means of implementing changes suggested by the survey results.

Presenting data

The original purpose of the survey will have a bearing on the emphasis of the final documentation of the results. Presenting the results of a survey, whether this is in a written form or in the form of an oral presentation, is the ultimate goal of the research. This is the opportunity for the researcher to deliver the results/conclusions/recommendations of the research and is the final essence of the project. Therefore it is important to interpret the findings so that their significance may be appreciated, to report the results accurately and to draw out any generalizations or projections that are relevant in a logical, cogent argument.

An important issue in the presentation of results is that the recipients should believe in their credibility and application. In order to achieve this it is important to adopt a style of writing that is consistent with the kinds of conclusions or generalizations that are being drawn from the data.

Planning and writing a report

Planning the report should include the collation of all the necessary material. A draft outline is useful to organize the material for the final report. A useful report outline includes the following sections:

1. Statement of the original aims/objectives of the survey.

2. Record of how the research was carried out/the methodology used.

3. Summary of the findings.

4. Recommendations/conclusions.

5. Detailed results.

6. Appendices:

   copies of the questionnaire

   letters

   tables

Further action

Management must be committed to take action on the survey findings as quickly as possible. Expectations of action and the change will have built up in the respondents during the survey process. It is important not to lose momentum and credibility by just filing the results, otherwise this valuable exercise in upward communication will be wasted.

References

Babbie, E. R. (1973) *Survey Research Methods*, Wadsworth, Belmont, CA.

Jolliffe, F. R. (1986) *Survey Design and Analysis*, Ellis Horwood, Chichester.

Reeves, T. K. and Harper, D. (1981) *Surveys at Work: Student project manual*, McGraw-Hill, London.

6

Negotiating

INTRODUCTION

Taking note of the media coverage of union 'negotiating', you are likely to get the impression that negotiating is another way of saying 'engaging in conflict', yet the Oxford Dictionary defines 'negotiate' as: 'confer with another person with a view to compromise or agreement . . . to arrange or bring about.'

In other words, negotiating means taking action in order to achieve a situation acceptable to both parties. It occurs when the interests of a person or group are dependent upon the actions of another person or group who also have interests to pursue and whose respective interests are pursued by co-operative means.

A negotiation is a meeting between two parties, and the objective is to reach an agreement over issues which:

- are important in both parties' views
- may involve conflict between the parties
- need both parties to work together to achieve their objective

In a work context, negotiations constantly occur between employers and employees (wages, conditions of service); between sales representatives and buyers on prices and contracts; between departments on resource allocation. Negotiations need not have a winner and a loser: in every negotiation there are opportunities to be creative in using social skills and effective communication to bring both parties together towards a positive outcome that is in their mutual interest.

As George Bernard Shaw so aptly said:

We must not stay as we are, doing always what was done last time, or we shall stick in the mud.

Shaw's statement very aptly sets the scene which should be the basis for all negotiating – the provision of attitudes and an environment which will enable the issues to be discussed positively and constructively and with a view to resolution.

As the negotiator, your aim should be actively to achieve the desired result or in simpler words – to do business! The essence of negotiating effectively lies in careful preparation, establishing a collaborative climate, and using skills of interpersonal communication, critical thinking and analysis. If negotiators can achieve satisfaction of their own personal needs in the negotiating situation, if they can equate these with achieving the best outcome for their party, there is a basis for success.

Like so many aspects of communication, the success of negotiation can be substantially enhanced by approaching it from the correct point of view, and the following sections will lay down the appropriate guidelines under the following headings:

The subject under negotiation

Preparing for negotiation

Achieving the right climate

Negotiating styles

Finding solutions

Fall-back situations

Behaviour in negotiation

The subject under negotiation

While you may be clear about what issues you are being asked to negotiate, you should also be aware that there are some contexts where negotiation is inappropriate:

- Negotiating trading terms when strict terms are already laid down by the company.
- Negotiating issues which ignore legislation relating to race, sex or other discrimination.

- Negotiating breaches of company disciplinary procedures.
- Negotiating over a company decision which you have been asked to announce.
- Negotiating when all parties are not present.

Having ascertained that the issue is one which you *can* negotiate, you should then determine what you wish to achieve, and with whom, at each stage of the negotiation. Know what your objectives are, what factors are vital, and which ones might be abdicated in certain circumstances. Only when you have defined your objectives can you begin to prepare for the negotiations.

CHECKLIST 6.1   NEGOTIATING OBJECTIVES

---

1. What are our objectives? What outcomes do we want?
2. Are our objectives specific, timed, and measurable?
3. Do we have a fall-back position?
4. If we were in their shoes, what would our position be? Do we know their objectives? If not, how can we find out?
5. What demands are they likely to make? What concessions are we likely to have to give?
6. Do they know our objectives? Our fall-back position?
7. How much room for manoeuvre is there between our two positions?
8. How strongly are we committed to our objectives as a negotiating team?
9. As representatives, how strongly are our constituents behind us?
10. What is the best outcome we can realistically hope for? The worst we would be prepared to settle for?

Preparing for negotiation

Effective preparation is vital if you are to achieve the best results. Successful negotiators have broad and specific objectives and have planned how to achieve these before sitting down at the negotiating table. They can then be proactive and direct the negotiators towards achieving these objectives rather than being merely reactive to the other party's proposals. Beware, however, of having tunnel vision about your objectives or strategy. Be flexible! Try to identify clearly the areas of agreement, and potential areas of conflict where co-operation and/or compromise can be used to reach agreement. If not, you may find yourself with very little room to manoeuvre during the negotiation itself, and this can result in either you or the other party feeling backed into a corner, or becoming frustrated. This leads to negative attitudes developing into non-co-operation and eventual refusal to reach agreement, because of perceived lack of consideration of arguments or feelings.

Do not, at the preparation stage, become too committed to some unchangeable action or policy. If the other party becomes aware of this, and that this is the only outcome that you are seeking and will accept, the negotiation will be compromised as soon as it begins. Synergy and successful negotiating situations are more likely to occur when you are willing (and able) to rethink your objectives and strategy during the negotiation itself in the light of information and attitudes revealed to you by the other party. A win/lose or lose/lose situation benefits no one: the winners and losers have to live with each other afterwards, and future negotiations may be prejudiced by either of these outcomes.

With time on your hands, try to get to know as much about the other negotiating party as possible:

- Is he/she independent or part of a team?
- Is he/she authorised to make decisions without referring back?
- Can he/she deliver, and if not, who can?
- What type of person is he/she? How experienced a negotiator?
- What type of approach is likely to achieve the best results?
- What are his/her interests likely to be and in what order of priority?
- What type of behaviour can you expect from this person?

Your bargaining power

Power, as it is perceived and used by both parties, can determine the outcome to a large extent. What are the offers or demands being made? What are the consequences to each party of rejection or acceptance of them? Does rejection (or acceptance) mean more to one party than to the other? How then should you react to the proposals? When you have assessed your bargaining power, go back and reconsider your original objectives.

Your negotiating strategy

The best strategy is the one which is effective in the context of the negotiating situation itself. If you fail to find the right strategy, you are unlikely to achieve your desired outcome.

- How can you change the other party's expectations?

- How can you get information from them, e.g. their commitment to their objectives, the importance to them of achieving them, their fall-back positions?

- How can you increase your bargaining power? By pre-negotiation conditioning? What strategies can you use to counter theirs?

- What sorts of strategies can you use?

- How can you best structure the agenda? For structuring the other party's expectations? Do you want to treat the items singly or as a package?

CHECKLIST 6.2   NEGOTIATING TACTICS

Once you have determined your objectives, your broad strategy and your relative bargaining power, how are you going to approach the negotiation itself? What tactics will you use?

1. Do you open by putting your demands on the table first? Or draw these out?

2. How can you gain the initiative?

    (a) by being assertive or unwilling to compromise?

    (b) by using reasoned arguments, committed to a fair outcome?

3. What contingency plans do you have to cope with the unexpected? Break off negotiations? Go back to your constituents for further guidance? Agree, but renege on the agreement later? What are the consequences of each of these actions in the short term/in the long term? In terms of your credibility and bargaining power with the other party?

4. What do you know about the individuals in the other team? Their strengths and weaknesses? Their personalities? Have they a specific style that you can disrupt?

5. How good are they at bluffing? How good are you? Is bluff a useful tactic in this particular situation?

6. Are you certain you can separate the facts from opinions, assumptions, hearsay? Will the other party accept your 'facts'?

7. How best can you sell the benefits of your proposals?

8. How best can you sell the unpleasant consequences to the other party if they reject your proposals?

9. How will you deal with the weaknesses in your proposals/arguments?

10. Will you be rational/logical in your argument, or appeal to emotions? A bit of both? Where is it best to use one or the other approach?

11. What is the best sequence for introducing your proposals? How will you most effectively use the time available?

12. Where do you want the negotiations to be held? Your base? Their base? Neutral ground?

13. Whom do you want to chair the meeting? You or them?

14. How realistic should your opening demand be? Do you want to make an opening demand? Or adopt a problem-solving approach?

15. At what stages should you give information? Or withhold it?

16. Do you have the technical knowhow/skills to negotiate effectively on the issues? Where can you get support in these areas if necessary?

17. Have you the interpersonal/social skills to manage your relationship with the other party?

BE FLEXIBLE!

Brief your negotiating team

Brief them on the strategy, the roles and tasks you want them to perform during the negotiation: who takes notes, who acts as chairperson, who deals with interruptions, how to deal with conflict techniques (e.g. misquoting, discrediting, ignoring contributors, etc.) and who should control the pace of the negotiation.

This knowledge will enable you to plan your approach to the negotiation and make you aware of areas where you may have to give way, and other areas where you will be able to gain. It will also prepare you for likely 'dirty tricks' which might be introduced into the discussions. Make sure your team members are briefed on how to behave under pressure, and that they know the importance of non-verbal communication.

The negotiation

Negotiating interests

Time and again media reports contain the emotive words, 'deadlock-ed', 'demands', etc., and for the most part such situations occur because the negotiating parties are obstinately stating, and sticking to, positions from which they refuse to budge; clearly, the negotiations can go absolutely nowhere in these circumstances. More often than not this stance is accompanied by the interests of the parties being totally ignored, with the result that the final settlement satisfies no-one.

The golden rule is therefore always to *negotiate interests* rather than positions: *do not adopt any position unless it is truly advantageous to those interests*. Beware of trying to achieve your personal objectives in a negotiating situation – you are acting as a representative and not as an individual. Your constituents' objectives come first.

Once you have decided what your party's interests are it is critical to try to determine what the interests of the other party are, and this can normally be achieved by asking questions such as:

What would you like to achieve?
When do you think this should begin?
How should we aim to put this into operation?
What do you think we should do?

Responses to your enquiries may be immediately forthcoming, but there will be times when you may have to adopt more probing questions in order to arrive at a clear understanding – it is often the case that such an exercise helps the other party to clarify its objectives if it has not taken the time to do so beforehand.

Achieving the right climate

The climate in negotiations has a major effect on progress to positive outcomes. Try to create the climate you want.

'Climate' is formed in a very short time: seconds or minutes. It is affected by the past relationships between the parties, their present expectations, the attitudes, perceptions and skills they bring to the situation. It is affected by the context of the meeting, the location, the seating arrangements, the degree of formality, the 'domestic' arrange-ments.

In the ice-breaking period you should strive to create a climate that is cordial, collaborative, brisk and businesslike. Friendly verbal communication and non-verbal cues (such as eye contact) can help enormously to create conditions for people to be motivated to collaborate: the converse also applies.

These opening moves (as in chess) set the climate for the way in which the negotiation is likely to progress and also helps you to gain information about the character, attitude and intentions of the other party. Try to look for cues which give you an indication of their experience, skills and negotiating style. Experienced negotiators will search for co-operation on neutral topics; negotiators with power needs will probe to identify your strengths and weaknesses, priorities and concerns. These cues enable you to assess and consider how you may have to vary your strategy in the later stages of the negotiations.

Negotiating styles

The style we use can build on the climate created at the start or it can change the climate from one of collaboration to one of competition, conflict and personal skirmishes.

Having identified and agreed at the beginning the purpose of the negotiation, the procedures and processes to be used, the time constraints, the positions of each party, we need jointly to identify the issues to be discussed and the interests on which to negotiate. The types of style we can use can be described in two dimensions as **direction** and **strength**.

Direction refers to the way we handle information. We can **push**: give information, make proposals, ignore other people's contributions, criticize, act as an irritator – all valid tactics dependent on the nature and context of the negotiation. Or we can **pull**: ask questions to obtain information, ask for suggestions, check for understanding, ask for clarification, state our feelings.

Strength refers to the flexibility we use to move from our initial positions. We can act **hard**: we want to win at all costs, we will not concede or retract, will not accept offers – we aim high! Or we can act **soft**: we concede, we waver, we find it difficult to say no, we accommodate – we aim low. We may act hard on some issues and soft on others: this gives a clear indication of where our preferred outcome priorities lie.

Bidding tactics

Bidding on substantive issues in negotiations is like bidding in poker – we bid on the exposed cards (information) and on our assessment of the other party as people and our perception or estimation of the importance of a positive outcome to them. We can bid high or low.

- A high bid has the advantage that you might just get away with it! It tells the other party how much you want, but still leaves room for manoeuvring. However, there is always the risk with a high bid that the other party might just walk out. They may see you as being bloody-minded and you could prejudice future bargaining relationships.

- A low bid may get you a quick settlement. The other party feels like collaborating, as they perceive it to be realistic (in their terms). However, once you have bid low, you will have difficulty in raising your bid afterwards and you may have problems with your constituents, who may feel you have 'sold them down the river'. You give yourself little room for movement.

You would therefore normally bid high in your opening bid, but no higher than you could rationally defend.

Bidding clarifies where the differences lie between the parties and creates a basis from which they can move forward to resolve these differences. The tactics you can use are to focus on a specific detail, or to trade off one item against another, or to move forward on a broad front. It is therefore always important to be able to identify common ground rather than differences. You should acquire the following control skills:

- Review progress: where are we in relation to the objectives stated at the beginning?

- Clarify problems: make sure everyone is aware of the real differences.

- Show agreement: keep a collaborative climate by acknowledging or agreeing points made by the other party.

- Summarize: what have we agreed so far? How do we feel now?

- Monitor progress against elapsed time: remember that people's concentration drops rapidly after about twenty minutes. Try to achieve agreement on points or stages of the negotiation before their concentration wavers – if necessary, take a break, adjourn after summarizing where you are, and start again.

The skills you need to develop are those of creating and maintaining interest, keeping concentration going, time-watching and building relationships of mutual respect and trust. These will help you negotiate effectively and achieve a positive outcome.

CHECKLIST 6.3   THE NEGOTIATION PROCESS

Consider the following process issues:

1.   Shared/unshared perception: what is the problem? Check perceptions of both parties.
2.   Hard v. soft approach.
3.   Stubborn v. flexible position / trust v. mistrust.
4.   Balancing air time v. listening.
5.   Competition v. co-operation.
6.   Willingness/unwillingness to compromise/trade off/make concessions.
7.   Going for a 'win/lose' outcome v. a 'win/win' one.
8.   Use of adjournments to regroup forces/obtain more information/redesign strategy or tactics/ redefine objectives.
9.   Use of non-verbal signals.
10.   Use of silence.
11.   Relative authority of each party's negotiating teams to conclude agreements.
12.   Offer of arbitration as a tactical device/to demonstrate commitment and trust/because you know you can influence the arbitrator.

Finding solutions

Solutions can only be found when both parties are prepared 'to do business' and this means that both parties are able and willing to move forward. Sometimes you may find that the other party is unable and unwilling to move or respond and this is where you will need to ask 'why not?' Is it because of their stance or perhaps the result of what you are asking? If the latter is the case you will need to review your interests to ascertain the reason for the blockage, and try to seek an alternative way to progress.

Another reason why the other party may not be willing to proceed could be because of some code of behaviour or loyalty which he/she feels towards colleagues, and you may have to find a way of enabling him/her to 'save face' if that code has to be broken: by making it easier for him/her to agree to your terms you can often achieve a quick solution to the problem.

Having determined what your interests are, you should be able and prepared to:

1. State your objectives clearly and firmly (though not aggressively), without apology or any suggestion that there is room for compromise.

2. Discuss the issues objectively in a polite (if possible, friendly) and businesslike manner, maintaining control of your emotions at all times. As George Herbert once said: 'Be calm in arguing; for fierceness makes error a fault, and truth discourtesy; calmness is great advantage.'

3. Avoid an apologetic or insecure stance. Say, 'I cannot accept anything less than . . .', instead of, 'I would really prefer not to accept . . .'; and say, 'You are putting me in a difficult position' rather than 'I feel that I might be in a difficult position'. In other words, be firm while being polite and courteous, and never say 'may' when you mean 'must', and never say 'think' when you mean 'know'. **Say what you mean**.

4. Avoid a 'soft option' since it will almost certainly not look after your interests and will probably produce a less effective solution.

When seeking a solution your aim should be to allow both sides to win, or at worst declare a draw. If we use the analogy of who should get the cake, the options become:

LOSE/LOSE	Take the cake away so neither party gets it.
WIN/LOSE	Give it to one party or cut it unevenly.
DRAW	Cut the cake down the middle.
WIN/WIN	Make two cakes or a much larger one.

Clearly, the first two options would leave one or both of the parties dissatisfied with the result and lead to further unease or conflict in the future. You should therefore remember:

Never, in the heat of the moment, create a 'lose/lose' situation.

Avoid a 'win/lose' situation whenever you can.

Accept nothing less than a 'draw'.

Aim at a 'win/win' solution.

The self-fulfilling prophecy is likely to occur. If parties go into a negotiating situation with an attitude that a win/lose outcome will occur, it most likely will! People tend to discount cues and information that contradict their preconceived ideas; they select only those which reinforce their preconceptions. If people negotiate with a win/win attitude, a positive outcome for both parties is more likely to occur.

Look first for shared interests and then for compatible interests by these methods:

- Creating a climate in which both parties are able to put forward as many relevant ideas for a solution as possible.
- Avoiding making judgments until all ideas have been introduced.
- Concentrating on the problem, rather than on the people involved.
- Knowing what you are trying to achieve.
- Not responding to rhetorical questions used for bolstering position rather than addressing interests.

Finally, do not lose your temper or provoke your partners to do so, since this will not produce solutions and neither side can benefit; however, it is sometimes necessary to allow the other party to 'let off steam' and this may result in shouting or worse, but the result will be to allow him/her to calm down. Do not retaliate – it is better to remain quiet and let their lack of control be of service to you.

It is not a sign of weakness to receive abuse without responding, and you will often find it beneficial to help the other party to regain control since you will then be able to proceed more positively. If both parties lose their temper, the meeting should be adjourned to give you both time to cool off, though when you suggest an adjournment it should be on the grounds of preserving the progress you have both made rather than because of the behaviour you are displaying.

Once you are in discussion, always listen to understand what is being said to you, and speak to be understood. This will give you the best chance of avoiding misunderstandings which can prolong the negotiating procedure.

Fall-back situations

It would be naïve to suggest that by applying all the advice given in this chapter you will float smoothly through all negotiations and emerge joyful and triumphant at the end. There may be times when your opposing negotiator has also read this book and will be equally prepared, with clear objectives, producing a convincing argument as to his/her interests!

When this situation arises, and it is not possible to move the negotiations forward however much you both wish to achieve a solution, you will need to have your BATNA already worked out and ready to bring forward. (It should be noted that this situation often occurs when you are in the position of *having* to reach an agreement, and your partner is aware of that.)

BATNA is your 'Best Alternative To a Negotiated Agreement' (Fisher and Urg, 1981, *Getting to Yes*, Hutchinson) and its existence will probably allow you to continue to negotiate with some flexibility:

- By knowing what the best alternative is to being unable to agree on your prime interest.
- By assessing the value of your BATNA in relation to the best offer available.
- By comparing the two continually.

This process should prevent you from accepting what you should reject, or rejecting what you should accept.

Whether you are negotiating on a BATNA or against a 'bottom line', you should always remain open-minded about possible solutions and fully aware of the consequences of those proposed, or indeed the consequences of failing to reach an agreement. You do not *have* to agree, and it may be that the correct thing to do is to 'fail to agree' if that is more acceptable than the best offer presented to you.

It follows that it makes good sense to try to find out what your partner's BATNA might be, as accurately as possible, since it may be more acceptable to you to move in that direction than to have to fall back to your own BATNA position.

Fall-back position

Assess your strategy and modify your tactics to try to reach a BATNA acceptable to both parties. You know your BATNA: say, in a price negotiation with a buyer, you are prepared (and permitted) to offer up to 20% discount on an offered price. You open the bidding by offering an 10% discount, which is rejected out of hand, and receive a demand

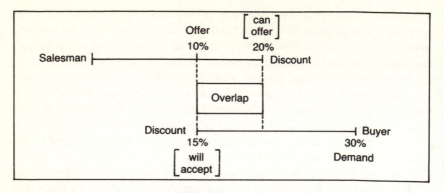

Figure 6.1   Assessing a fall-back position

for 30%. In fact, the other party is willing to accept a 15% discount – but you do not know this. There is an overlap in the fall-back positions, so the optimum outcome falls within both parties' individual assessment of a realistic agreement and an outcome between 15% and 20% discount can be agreed (see Figure 6.1). Whereabout this lies depends on several factors:

- The negotiating skills of the salesman and the buyer.
- How much the salesman needs to make the sale.
- How urgently the buyer requires the goods.

However, where the salesman's fall-back position is a 15% discount, and the buyer will accept no less than a 20% discount, there is no overlap, and the negotiation has no chance of succeeding.

It is important, both in overlap and no-overlap situations, to try to keep the shape of the deal fluid, to help both parties to search creatively for ways to put the agreement together to their mutual advantage. Adding an attractive service package to a 12% discount offer to the buyer could clinch the deal for the salesman if he can sell the long-term benefits to such a deal to the buyer. Offering repeat orders of a size which would be beneficial to the salesman's company from a production economies of scale viewpoint might swing the salesman to accept a 23% discount demand.

Keep the whole package in view when you are negotiating, and be prepared to be creative to reach agreement. But do not introduce new proposals at a very late stage – this can be disruptive and is likely to upset the co-operative climate you have already established.

Remember that most negotiations are not just one-off affairs.

Employer/employee, salesman/buyer – these are examples of long-term relationships which existed before the negotiation began, and will have to continue and be maintained long after the negotiation has finished. And there will in the future be other negotiations between the parties. So make sure that both parties go away from the negotiations feeling they have achieved something positive. If one party feels it has been exploited in the process, resentment will fester; implementation of the agreement will be done under duress; and the negotiators will lose credibility and become scapegoats for the dissatisfaction of their constituents. Remember that you may face more reluctant and aggressive negotiators next time – who are out to 'screw' you! Therefore look at the outcome and its implications from the point of view of the other party, too. If you don't, you are closing your eyes to potential future conflict.

Closing negotiations

When you have reached an agreement on the outcome (assuming you have), the agreement should be written down and signed by both parties – this allows for no misunderstanding or misinterpretation later. It is important that you agree jointly on how the publication of the agreement should be made: if it is done bilaterally and simultaneously, you are likely to get joint commitment for the agreement.

Real commitment is critical for successful implementation. So to make it stick, a record of what actions each party has to take, when, in what sequence, and how to monitor progress, should be made before the negotiation meeting closes. You may also need to have further meetings to monitor progress and clear up administrative details which you were not able to cover completely during the negotiation itself. Check the following:

- Are we all clear about what has been agreed?
- Are we all committed to the agreement?
- Do we need to meet again to clear up any minor (or major) points? When?
- How do both parties feel about the agreements we have made? Were they fair? Do we feel happy? Acrimonious? Bloody-minded? Sick?

After the negotiation is over it is easy to walk away and forget all about it and the performance of the team until the next negotiation takes place. Do not do that! Review what happened before, during, and after the negotiation. If you do not, you will not have learned anything that can make you a better negotiator next time.

Review your planning and preparation; how you conducted the process itself; note any variations in the outcomes from your anticipated ones, and why; how your team performed in their roles; which sorts of behaviour were productive, and which were counter-productive; and consider what you need to develop, especially in the skills area, before you sit down to a negotiation again.

Behaviour in negotiations

This chapter began by pointing out the misconceptions about negotiating which are portrayed by the media. And there are those who will prefer to stick to the positional, hard-line style, unaware of a more effective alternative. If you are unfortunate enough to be faced with a 'hard case', there are certain guidelines to which you should endeavour to adhere:

1. Maintain a polite and businesslike approach.

2. Do not retaliate when abusive behaviour is used.

3. Continue to negotiate on your interests, even if the other party is not doing so – ask for reasons for their stance (even if you know that there are none) and try to expose the weakness of their case by logical and reasoned discussion.

4. Invite ideas and criticism of your case, and suggest that your opponent try to look at the situation from your perspective.

5. Continually focus attention away from yourself and towards the issues under discussion.

6. Ignore unreasonable or personal attacks and respond by keeping silent; after a short silence try to refocus the discussion on the issues.

7. Instead of accepting bald statements, ask for objective criteria, reasons, explanations, back-up figures, precedents or summaries, even if you know they do not exist.

8. Show your enthusiasm for a fair solution and repeat your readiness to produce or agree objective criteria.

9. Listen for any sign of co-operation and then encourage it, welcome it, praise it, focus on it and make sure that you keep it 'on the table'.

10. Periodically summarize the areas where agreement has been reached and highlight the items which are still being negotiated, stressing your enthusiasm for the 'successful strides which have already been taken to reach agreement'.

11. Do not respond to the folowing tricks:
    - personal abuse, namecalling, etc.
    - totally misleading or deceitful comments, half-truths or rumours
    - rhetorical questions
    - brinkmanship
    - impossible/escalating demands
    - sarcasm
    - attempts to increase the stress on you
    - last-minute introduction of some other person to whom reference has to be made, when you had been told that you were negotiating with the decision maker.

12. If all else fails, be prepared to adjourn the discussion. Use the adjournment time to:
    - allow tempers to cool
    - review the points agreed and reconsider the items outstanding
    - take stock of the situation
    - carry out further checks on your negotiating partner(s)
    - seek any further approval or authorization which you might need.

CHECKLIST 6.4   KEY POINTS ABOUT NEGOTIATING

1. Negotiating is about power and influence, and agreeing on issues which generate conflict between the parties.
2. It does not have to be a win/lose situation.
3. Try to work towards a win/win situation. Both parties have to live with the agreements made and with each other afterwards.

4. Structure the negotiation to satisfy both parties.

5. Effective negotiation needs careful preparation.

6. You need to plan and identify best outcomes; what settlements are realistic; your BATNA and fall-back positions.

7. Your strategy should be flexible, to allow you to initiate or build on creative options which may appear.

8. The outcome of most negotiations depends to a large extent on the relative power of the partners involved. Try to build your bargaining power before the negotiation starts.

9. Bargaining power may vary across the issues being negotiated.

10. Development and use of negotiating skills can have major effects on the outcome.

11. Creating rapport and a collaborative climate at the beginning helps you move towards a positive outcome.

12. Look first for areas of agreement between the parties – there may be more than you realize.

13. Consider the other party's point of view first.

14. Identify the objectives of the individual negotiators (what are their hidden agendas?) and try to match them with your search towards satisfactory agreements.

15. Check that everyone knows what has been agreed, and who does what, and when, afterwards.

16. Review your performance and identify what you need to do better next time (both task and process).

Exercises in negotiating

Two situations are described below which require you to exercise the skills and techniques described in this chapter. They are common situations which any manager may face in his/her work context. Work through the exercises using the guidelines provided and consider what you can learn from your performance to develop your skills as an effective negotiator.

EXERCISE 6.1 NEGOTIATING A SALARY INCREASE

You are sure you are underpaid for the work you do. Your job description and accountabilities have changed enormously since you were appointed two years ago, due to the growth of the company, and the acquisition of other companies in the group has meant that you are having to work overtime and at weekends to maintain standards.

Your boss says he is constrained by the salary structure of the group and is also unsympathetic to your plea, although he has the authority to increase your salary to a level you would accept. He is not convinced that you are managing your time effectively, but is willing to talk to you regarding your situation.

1.   Prepare for negotiating over this issue with your boss.

2.   Work with two others in a role-play situation, one of whom takes the role of your boss, and the other observes what happens.

3.   Role-play the negotiation.

4.   Review the negotiation, with discussion initiated by the observer's feedback. Look especially at task and process skills.

5.   Consider what you can learn from this to make you a more effective negotiator.

EXERCISE 6.2   NEGOTIATING A NEW SALES AGREEMENT

You are the sales manager of an engineering components company. Your best salesman has informed you that a large customer has transferred his allegiance to another supplier; only vague reasons have been given. This decision has a major impact not only on the achievement of your sales budget, but also on the company's expansion plans. You decide to see the MD of the company involved to negotiate a new sales agreement which would be satisfactory to both parties.

1.   Prepare for this meeting.

2.   Role play this meeting with two others, one as MD of the other company, one as observer.

3.   Review the negotiation, using the observer's feedback as a basis for looking at task and process skills.

4.   What must you do to improve your effectiveness?

SUMMARY

From the information you have gained in this chapter you will know that negotiation is something which requires a great deal of preparation and which, even then, cannot be rushed. As Winston Churchill once said, 'It is a mistake to try to look too far ahead. The chain of destiny can only be grasped one link at a time.'

The advice which has been provided will help you to become a skilled negotiator – it will not unfortunately produce equal skills 'on the other side of the table'. You must therefore be prepared to take the lead in terms of personal control and professionalism, stating your intention to find a solution which is fair to everyone, and avoiding the sort of aggressive behaviour which you may yourself become subject to.

The sections in this chapter should enable you to work to the following checklist:

1. Prepare: know your objectives and the extent of your authority.

2. Plan your BATNA: just in case you need it.

3. Check out your negotiating partner: try to determine his/her interests and what his/her BATNA might be.

4. Clearly state your intentions and your level of authority.

5. Negotiate only on interests.

6. Seek as many solution options as possible before making a decision.

7. Behave professionally at all times.

8. Be prepared to fail if failure is the best alternative: in some cases failure may be the best solution available.

To recap what was said at the beginning of the chapter: remember that your intention in negotiating any issue will be to reach 'compromise or agreement', and it is perhaps worth concluding with quotations from William Wrigley and Moshe Dayan:

1. When two men in business always agree, one of them is unnecessary.

2. If you want to make peace, you don't talk to your friends. You talk to your enemies.

7

Training for effective communication skills

Oh! This learning! What a thing it is!

William Shakespeare, *The Taming of the Shrew*

INTRODUCTION

Developing communication skills is like learning to play contract bridge. You need to learn the rules and the conventions. You also need a partner to practise with and you need to learn how well you are doing, so that you can improve on your areas of weakness in bidding or playing. And it is only with practice and feedback that you will develop into a good bridge player or an effective communicator. So the emphasis must be on empirical learning – learning by doing – and on receiving feedback.

The authors, in their book *The Essence of Successful Staff Selection*, have indicated that there are so many variables in the job situation, especially at managerial levels, that few jobs have identical requirements; no standard blend of managerial characteristics and abilities will meet all requirements and the 'syllabus' approach to training is misguided. The processes that managers have to pursue in the normal course of their work require qualities that can only be identified broadly, in terms of defined needs in knowledge and skills.

The starting point for determining the training approach should therefore be:

1. Knowledge: what knowledge is required now and in the future as regards the manager's own function, other functions, the industry, general management, and external trends and pressures.

131

2. Skills: what is required now and in the future as regards functional skills (e.g. financial, research, technical) problem solving skills (everything concerned with the use of intelligence) and human (everything concerned with personal relationships) skills.

Managerial work and communication

Managers work in a stimulus-reactive environment. The nature of their work is typically varied, spasmodic and brief, and they do a great quantity of work at an unrelenting pace. In general, they prefer to deal with specific issues, prefer verbal media, and to control to some degree their own activities. However, it is likely that managers will carry out their work, even in very similar jobs, in different ways, dependent on their choices concerning what to do and how to do it. These choices are influenced by the managers' own perceptions, preferences and personal characteristics.

Within their personal work contexts, managers work in three clearly identifiable roles which change rapidly from one to another because of the episodic nature of their work. These roles can be classified as interpersonal, informational, and decisional. However, to make effective decisions (allocating resources, dealing with problems, etc.) managers need to collect relevant information, and to collect information they require effective formal and informal communication with bosses, colleagues (often in other functions), subordinates, and contacts external to the organization.

So, to be effective managers, skilled in decision making (on which they are most frequently judged and appraised for salary and promotion), they need to be effective communicators. But as they make choices regarding their approach to individual jobs, the specific communication skills they need will vary from manager to manager, from job to job.

Training and development

Classically, the lines between training and development are blurred. You can debate the differences and similarities for as long as you could debate how many angels you could place on the head of a pin, but we differentiate between the two concepts in a very simple manner:

1. Training: a means of facilitating learning to improve performance in the job. It is concerned with *tactics*.

2. Development: a means of facilitating learning to improve performance in the present job and in future jobs, in relation to the total business effort and the policies that determine the direction of the business. It is concerned with *strategy*.

Development is therefore, in our view, more linked to a process of changing the individual as a person, rather than in the acquisition of specific required current knowledge and skills. Our approach to management development is therefore as follows:

1. Concentrate on what people do: tasks, accountabilities, problems.

2. Examine work relationships throughout the organization/unit.

3. Develop analytical methods that will disclose work problems and attitudes.

4. Concentrate effort on:
   (a) manager implementation
   (b) work-team activities

5. Use courses and programmes as a means to an end. They should be:
   (a) diagnostic
   (b) non-didactic

6. Gear development work to assist the organization to meet technological, organizational, social, cultural and environmental changes.

You will see that the first five items are equally applicable to our definition of training, whilst the sixth looks further ahead than the immediate future. So it should be when we talk about the development of communication skills. These skills, once learned and practised, will make an increasingly important contribution to the future effectiveness of the organization.

Learning

With any development activity at work, there are four basic components which need to be present for success. These are illustrated in

Figure 7.1. People must first of all have *the will to learn*. You can take a horse to water, but you cannot make it drink. If this is lacking, no matter how relevant, attractive, well designed your courses are, there will be no positive outcome.

If people want to learn, they must have *the opportunity to learn*. Nothing can be more frustrating, demotivating and demoralizing for people who have identified areas in which they are weak, and want to learn to do better, than to have no opportunity to do so. And by learning, we do not necessarily mean formal training or development courses: there are other, and sometimes more appropriate and relevant, ways of learning, as we will discuss later in this chapter.

People need *the opportunity to practise* what they have learned. Knowledge and skills atrophy with disuse. A manager who has been sent on a management development programme at a business school will more than likely return to work to find his in-tray full to overflowing. Demands for his advice, his operational know-how, the short-term requirements of his job will be great. What he has learned on the programme, the ideas he has bursting out of him, take a very low priority in his requirement to meet targets. And when he finds time to get round to thinking about what he has learned, his initial enthusiasm and motivation have eroded, and little change occurs. If organizations are to invest in learning, they *must* look for a return on their investment by giving the learner opportunities to practise what has been learned.

It is all very well to practise, but for learning to be internalized and reinforced, the learner needs to get feedback on his implementation of

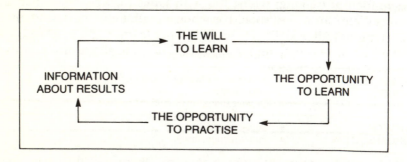

Figure 7.1 Development at work: basic components

that learning in his work context. He or she needs *information about results:*

1. Is he or she applying the knowledge gained correctly? Well? Badly? If so, why or why not?
2. What further learning/opportunities to practise are needed to ensure effective transfer of learning back into the work context and implementation? How can they be provided?
3. How can this learning be adapted/transferred to others to help them become more effective?

The approach to communication training

When we work at trying to develop effective organizational communication and individual communication skills, the questions raised by the four basic components (see Figure 7.1) become even more important. Organizations need to use a development approach to this training, as shown in Figure 7.2. By adopting this approach, organiza-

FOCUS	• Tasks, accountabilities, problems • Work relationships in unit and team • Intergroup and boss/subordinate relations
CONTENT	• Interpersonal and team membership skills • Joint problem solving, conflict management, helping
TARGET	• All levels • Senior management involvement in initial stages
STYLE	• Participant-centred (not trainer-centred) • Based on immediate experience
METHODS	• Informality; minimal lecture input • Flexible programme; self-diagnostic
RESULTS SOUGHT	• Individual: motivation to self-learning, awareness, adaptability • Organizational: contribution to results
VIEW OF ORGANIZATION	• Social system • Public responsibility

Figure 7.2   The development approach to training

135

tions are more likely to develop those skills which can be used effectively to improve individual and organizational performance.

Learning styles

You will note that in this approach, the style recommended is participant-centred, not trainer-centred. To design learning experiences which will be appropriate and relevant, you need therefore to identify the learner's preferred style of empirical learning.

Kolb *et al.* identified a model of learning and adaptation processes consistent with the ways in which we learn and develop and mature as people. The learning cycle shows how what we do can be translated into theories which we can use to modify our approaches to new experiences, as illustrated in Figure 7.3.

Learning is a four-stage cycle. What we do gives us a basis for looking back and analyzing what worked and what did not. From this analysis we can form general ideas about our experiences. We can then test out these general ideas in practice, and modify and revise them to fit work situations/experiences we will face in the future.

However, we all have our preferred style of learning, developed through our personal characteristics, our past experience, and our present environment. Some people emphasize particular learning approaches over others: some like to be active, some reflective, some prefer theoretical approaches, some analytical. By identifying your target audience's learning styles, you can help them learn more effectively (and quickly) by designing programmes which are congruent with these styles. Where we are considering the development of communication skills, we are trying to make managers more people-orientated, reducing conflict and disagreement, and promoting socially interactive skills. The emphasis in the learning experiences should be on concrete experience (learning by doing; exercises, role-plays; simulations, etc.) and on observations and reflections (looking back, analyzing what has been done, considering implications). But by identifying individual managers' preferred learning styles, you may have to adopt your approach to match these, while gradually moving into the style which is most appropriate for the achievement of your learning objectives – developing effective communication skills.

At Cranfield School of Management we have found that the learning styles of the MBA full-time students lean towards preferring an abstract, theoretical approach; while the part-time MBA students are

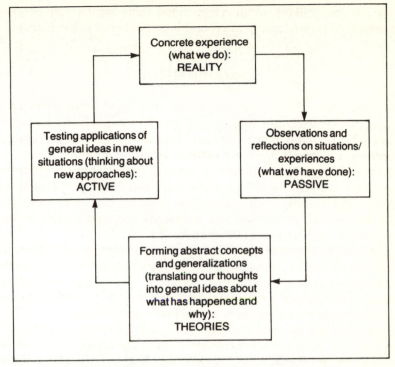

Figure 7.3 Kolb's experimental learning model

more concerned with considering how to apply their concepts in practice. This means that we approach the design of learning experiences for the two programmes slightly differently, to take into consideration the differences in the students' preferred learning styles. So it should be for organizations planning development for their managers. Be flexible!

Designing communication skills programmes

Communication skills programmes are of two kinds: (a) on the job and (b) off the job. In both cases, you have to work to a model as shown in Figure 7.4. The steps incorporated in it are described below:

1. *Define training objectives:* what are you trying to achieve? Why? What training strategies should you adopt?

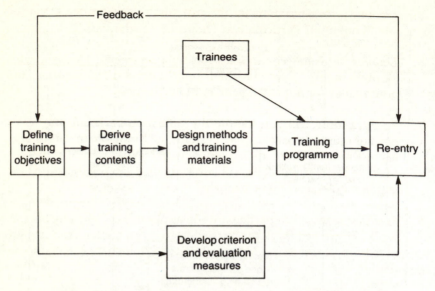

Figure 7.4   Designing a communications training programme

2. *Develop criteria:* how are you going to evaluate the programme?
    How can you relate future performance to the experience/learning
    on the programme itself? How can you develop quantitative
    measures of evaluation? Qualitative measures? What rewards can
    you link to improved performance?

3. *Derive training contents:* what are the key issues which need to
    be addressed? What is the target audience? What level/com-
    petence of participants? What experience of learning do they have?
    What is their attitude to learning? How long should the pro-
    gramme be? On the job/off the job?

4. *Design methods and training materials:* how will you achieve your
    objectives? What methods/learning styles do *you* want to use?
    What are the *learners'* preferred learning styles? Are they con-
    gruent? What modifications do you need to incorporate? What
    learning experiences do you feel will move the participants
    towards achieving your objectives? CCTV (Closed Circuit Televi-
    sion)? What materials will you use? How competent are your
    trainers?

5. *Training programme:* how best to structure the programme? Modular? Sequential? Participative? Didactic? Residential? How long?

6. *Trainees:* who has communication training needs? How did you identify them? Why train them now? Did you choose them for potential or for improving current effectiveness?

7. *Re-entry:* how will you handle the transition back into the work environment? What support systems will you set up? Will you leave the trainees to their own devices? What opportunities to practise the learned skills will you provide as an organization? Or is this merely a cosmetic exercise?

8. *Feedback:* feedback to participants on application of learning back at work? How? Feedback to course designers on content and design of learning experiences? How effective? What changes need to be made?

A basic tenet to remember is that when filling in a swamp you do not start by throwing dirt into the middle – you start at the edges and move in slowly and progressively. So it is with training in communication skills. You use a progressive approach. Skills development does not happen overnight. It takes time, and practice, and lots of lessons learned from mistakes, and perseverance to become more effective. Technical knowledge can be assimilated quickly – even by just reading the right text books. Human and social skills, which incorporate changes in attitudes, values and beliefs, require much time, support and constructive feedback for proficiency to develop.

A factor which seems to have been forgotten in the design of many programmes is this: training and development is about learning – but also about *enjoyment*! Managers are more likely to learn effectively if they are enjoying themselves.

Four basic communication skills

Managers, to be effective, need to develop four basic communication skills, and any training or development programme should incorporate them. These skills can be learned on the job or on formal programmes, but require continual practice and reinforcement so that they become part of a manager's 'tool box' when interacting with other people. They are:

1. Listening, and giving and receiving feedback.
2. Assertiveness.
3. Resolving conflict.
4. Solving problems.

Listening

We discussed listening, and especially active listening, in Chapter 1. If we do not listen, we receive distorted or garbled messages. The information on which we make decisions is therefore of minor value to us, and affects our effectiveness. We need to learn to listen for all cues, verbal and non-verbal, which, interpreted accurately, will give us complete understanding of messages being sent.

Giving and receiving feedback

These are skills which we tend to overlook as we feel generally that we are pretty good in these areas. However, generally we are not! To establish and build on relationships we need to obey certain rules in our social interactions which will help us to improve. Most people find both giving and receiving feedback, handling praise and criticism, equally difficult – the result is that we often only hear and listen when there is a real problem.

Here are some hints for improving the provision of feedback:

1. *Comment on specific actions:* say 'You sorted out that awkward problem very well' instead of 'You are good with difficult problems'. Equally, say 'You didn't meet your sales targets this month' rather than 'when are yc ʾ ever going to meet your targets?'

2. *Give reasons for your comments:* 'pointing out the implications for not giving the discount made it very clear why you couldn't do so.

3. *Concentrate on behaviour which can be changed*, which is within the control of the other person, rather than make personal comments about the individual.

4. *Be descriptive, not evaluative.*

5. *Express opinions as opinions, not facts.*

6. *Be constructive, not destructive.*

7. *Avoid loaded terms* which produce emotional reaction/defences.

8. *Giving praise:* genuine praise is more likely to be accepted if it is for better-than-normal performance and if it is given straight to the performer, rather than beating about the bush.

9. *Giving criticism:* do not put down people in front of others when you have described the facts; seek solutions jointly with the other person in private.

10. *Disagreeing with others:*
    (a) State your disagreement clearly: 'No, I disagree with . . .'
    (b) Be doubtful in a constructive way: 'The difficulty I see is, how can we get round the constraints?'
    (c) Be willing to change your opinion if more facts emerge.
    (d) Give reasons for your disagreement.
    (e) Recognize that others may have different points of view from yours.

11. *Refusing requests:*
    (a) Keep your reply short, do not ramble on justifying yourself.
    (b) Give reasons if you want to, but do not invent excuses.
    (c) Do not apologize profusely.
    (d) Ask for more information if you need it.
    (e) Ask for more time to decide if you need it.

Here are some hints on how to receive feedback:
1. Listen carefully.
2. Try not to let your hackles rise, your defences build.
3. Note areas of question/disagreement.
4. Paraphrase what you hear.
5. Check your perception of what you hear.
6. Ask for clarification/examples.
7. Do not over-react to feedback.
8. Evaluate its accuracy and potential value to you.

Active listening and feedback go hand in hand. They help to give and receive messages of greater clarity and understanding.

Assertiveness

How can you impress another person without necessarily upsetting him/her? How can you be forceful yet sufficiently sensitive to the other's feelings? The answer is, by being assertive. Each of us has our own personal space, both physical and psychological.

'Full thirty inches from my nose
The boundary of my person goes'

wrote W. H. Auden, and although the distance may differ from individual to individual, from culture to culture, the concept still applies.

The size of this personal space is influenced by our values, emotions, ideas and views about the world. People have a right to those values and do not thank others for encroaching on their personal territory. Assertiveness is a means of making an impact on other individuals without encroaching on their personal arena: it is a means of influencing others without damaging your interpersonal relationships.

Assertiveness lies between submissive and aggressive behaviour (see Figure 7.5). When you are submissive, you are unwilling or unable to express honest feelings, needs, values, personal concerns. You let other people violate your personal space and crush your rights. When you are aggressive, you tend to walk on other people. You impose your points of view and values on them and express your feelings at the expense of theirs. You are likely to generate resistance in others by blocking their demands or views, and have difficulty in getting them to make commitments.

Being assertive lets you say what you want, without overwhelming or abusing other people. You are clear about your own position and let other people know this, but can also accept that they may have other views and so may wish to negotiate their position accordingly.

Assertiveness training is a critical element in developing communication skills. It helps in all the following ways:

• Open, honest communication.
• Learning to relax and reduce anxiety.
• Getting more of your needs accepted.
• Learning social skills that form closer interpersonal relationships.

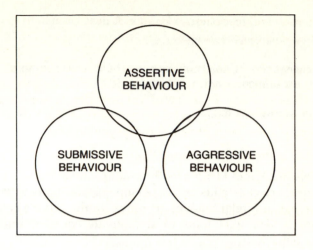

Figure 7.5 Assertiveness

- Taking responsibility for what happens in your life – at home, as well as at work.
- Making more decisions and free choices.
- Recognizing that you have certain rights and your own personal value system.
- Protecting yourself from being taken advantage of by other people.

EXERCISE 7.1

Here are some examples of assertiveness situations. How would you deal with them? You can also role-play them with a colleague and have an observer give you both feedback.

- Admitting you have made a mistake.
- Dealing with critical customers.
- Disagreeing with your boss.
- Asking others not to smoke.
- Giving an opinion at a meeting.
- Criticizing others' work.
- Asking subordinates to do unpleasant work.
- Responding to personal attacks (verbal, not physical!).

- Being asked to do something outside your job description.
- Dealing with persistent salesmen.

1. What changes do you need to make in your behaviour to be more assertive/less aggressive/less submissive?

2. How can you achieve this?

Assertive behaviour is more likely to alter someone else's behaviour and less likely to violate his or her personal space; there is little risk of damaging existing relationships or reducing the other's self-esteem; and there is less likelihood to demotivate, or risk uncontrolled defensive behaviour.

To improve the likelihood of success in an assertive approach, the following procedure should be adopted:

1. Prepare thoroughly beforehand.
2. Send your assertive message.
3. Listen actively and reflectively to the defensive response.
4. Recycle the process, if necessary.
5. Focus on the solution.

Managers need to develop assertiveness skills to become effective communicators.

Resolving conflict
Conflicts, tensions, problems with individuals or groups are inevitable in organizations. People are different: they have their own views on issues, their own approaches to solving problems. Interpersonal conflict arises just as much because of the manner in which discussions take place as from disgreement on specific issues. People can end up still disliking each other even after they have agreed on an issue, simply because of the way in which the negotiations were constructed. The question then is whether they will do what they have agreed. Are they committed to doing it? If not, this will eventually lead to further conflict.

To gain greater collaboration and commitment, you should consider these approaches to conflict situations:

1. Use active and reflective listening:
   (a) to improve understanding of each other's positions and views of the situation/problem;
   (b) to generate trust so that you can be open and honest with each other.

2. Use assertiveness skills:
   (a) to make a powerful impact on others;
   (b) to maintain their commitment to implement the agreed solution.

3. Reduce communication blockages between the parties:
   (a) do not try to dominate, to be aggressive, or to threaten;
   (b) do not make false judgments, e.g. confusing opinions with facts.

4. Concentrate on issues:
   (a) do not increase interpersonal tensions by criticism or negative feedback;
   (b) gather facts;
   (c) break down large issues into smaller workable units, then deal with each problem separately;
   (d) when you have reached agreement on one issue, consider how you can build on this to reach agreement on others.

5. Identify and appraise carefully the actions decided:
   (a) assess the consequences of these actions for both parties;
   (b) make sure you have a commitment for implementing the agreements; by whom, when, and how?
   (c) identify areas of potential future conflict and try to agree joint approaches to them now.

Solving problems

Solving problems is all about trying to find some form of mutual agreement about decisions and actions to be taken in problem situations. You, as manager, may have all the facts and resources at your disposal and may be therefore able to solve the problem without any discussion with other persons. This is not always the case!

You may have to share with others the problem, the facts, the feelings in the situation, so that you can make a high quality decision. It may also be necessary to gain the total commitment of others to the decision so that it will be implemented successfully. You will not necessarily achieve this if you make the decision by yourself.

The process of involving other people, especially your subordinates or colleagues, is simple:

1. You, as manager, share facts, feelings, values and opinions about the problem/situation with those who can contribute to a positive outcome.
2. You explore the situation from all points of view, seeking inputs from the others involved.
3. You identify all possible solutions.
4. You evaluate those solutions against the criteria you have agreed are necessary for a positive outcome.
5. You agree a solution which meets these criteria most closely, and which is appropriate to the situation rather than to any one person in particular (including yourself).

This sharing process, *genuinely* involving other people, means that everyone has the opportunity to influence the decision and is thus likely to be committed to it. This style is, however, time-consuming. You have to balance the time and cost involved in the process against the quality of the decision required and the degree of commitment and motivation it produces.

Integration of communication skills

When designing any communications skills programme, development of the four basic skills (see p. 139) should be included. Two further communication skills are important for managers to improve their effectiveness: counselling and coaching.

Counselling

Despite the efforts to place people in well-designed, highly-motivating jobs and to train them properly for those jobs, some people do behave in ways that cause problems for themselves and for the organization. These problems may be work-related, sometimes personal concerns and pressures which the individual brings to the job each day. Often a friendly suggestion or comment from the manager is all that is needed to remedy the problem. In more serious cases, the manager may have to counsel the employee to try to get him/her to change his/her behaviour or attitude.

Situations requiring counselling can arise in different ways:

1. An employee may sense that he/she is not doing too well on the job, or may be having problems at home which are affecting his/her work, so he/she comes to the manager for help (this only occurs where there already exists a good boss–subordinate relationship).

2. Employees may also come to their manager about problems they are having with other people. They want their manager to straighten out these other people. They may not see that they themselves are the problem. As far as they are concerned, they are OK, but those other people are not co-operating in the way they should.

3. An employee's behaviour or performance is not up to par, or is causing problems with others: yet he/she is not aware of it. In this case the manager must initiate the action and bring the problem to the attention of the subordinate.

To develop skills in counselling, you need to follow a systematic approach and keep certain basic principles in mind.

There are seven steps in effective counselling:

1. *Prepare for the counselling session*:
   (a) think through what you want to discuss;
   (b) give time for the employee to prepare;
   (c) ensure privacy and no interruptions.

2. *Define the purpose of the discussion.*

3. *State the problem*:
   (a) state what the employee has done or not done (*his/her performance*), not the sort of person he/she is (*his/her personality, his/her attitudes*);
   (b) try to find out and understand why the employee acted as he/she did (*gaining insight*), rather than evaluating his/her behaviour (*passing judgment*);

147

(c) make clear that your objective is to help the employee in the future (*develop him/her*), rather than discipline him/her for the past (*condemn him/her*).

4. *Get the employee's views*:
   (a) have the employee describe the situation as he/she sees it;
   (b) use appropriate questioning techniques;
   (c) restate/reflect what was said;
   (d) listen to what is said, and what is left unsaid;
   (e) do not jump to conclusions.

5. *Clarify the problems*:
   (a) have the employee state what he/she believes the problem really is;
   (b) reach agreement so that he/she sees it as his/her own problem.

6. *Help the employee develop a solution*:
   (a) ask for ideas;
   (b) share information;
   (c) agree specific courses of action.

7. *Follow-up*:
   (a) agree deadlines for actions;
   (b) check that these deadlines are met;
   (c) check that these actions are not causing further problems;
   (d) keep on counselling as needed.

Counselling is a confidential, non-directive, face-to-face relationship. It is about helping people to understand themselves and their feelings particularly with regard to specific problems. Any problem which is presented to you is often just superficial, a symptom, not a root cause. Your job is to help others to identify this before helping them to find their own ways of overcoming any difficulties they may face.

Coaching

You, as a manager, have a key role to play in the progress of your subordinates. One important way in which you do this is by coaching. Learning by 'sitting next to Nelly' is often not effective, the employee learning the bad habits along with the good, and perpetuating both. You need to have a genuine desire to act as coach and help your subordinates to improve their effectiveness in their jobs. By doing so, they will perform better, and you have a better chance of meeting your targets. However, coaching takes time, and many managers feel such pressure for short-term results that they sacrifice long-term development on this altar. It is a sacrifice to a false god.

The coaching process consists of three stages:

1. Identify opportunities for setting tasks which:
   (a) have specific learning targets;
   (b) are appropriate and relevant to the subordinate's job, learning abilities and development needs within the organization;
   (c) can be measured and monitored.

2. Set up monitoring systems:
   (a) measure progress against deadlines, skill development;
   (b) meet regularly to discuss and solve problems in a non-directive mode.

3. Measure task achievement against targets:
   (a) review performance when the task is complete;
   (b) identify blockages and facilitating factors;
   (c) jointly determine areas for future development.

Timing is critical for effective coaching. Do not try to coach when a subordinate is under extreme pressure of work – he or she must be motivated for effective progress to be made, and conditions and work situations must be favourable for successful coaching.

Communication skills required in coaching are:

- Setting clear targets which are attainable.
- Setting up and maintaining rapport in a close working relationship with the subordinate.
- Maintaining joint problem-solving.
- Empathy for the feelings of the person being coached.
- Active listening.

Remember, learning is only effective when:

- the learner sees value

149

- it is active, not passive
- the timing is right
- it is built on experience
- it is consolidated with practice
- the *learner* can monitor progress
- it is geared to the learner's capability and style

If these conditions pertain, and you develop your communication skills, you can become an effective coach. The progress of your subordinates reduces the time you have to spend on direct supervision, and you will thus have more time to work on the other important elements of your job.

SUMMARY

In this chapter we have considered approaches to developing effective communication skills. The roles the manager plays are heavily geared to the need to be an effective communicator. We have described a model of the learning process which is linked to managerial tasks and which provides a basis for developing communication skills programmes, and we have described the four basic communication skills: **listening** and **feedback skills**, **assertiveness**, **resolving conflict** and **problem solving.** Managers also require to develop the skills of **counselling** and **coaching**, and all learning experiences should be geared to the present and future needs of the employee, the job and the organization.

The development of the effective manager/communicator is a critical factor in the success of an organization. Develop your communication skills – and be sure to use and practise them. And finally: know yourself and others and you are halfway there!

> If you know the enemy and know yourself, you need not fear the result of a hundred battles. If you know yourself and not the enemy, for every victory gained you will also suffer a defeat. If you know neither the enemy nor yourself, you will succumb in every battle.
>
> Sun Tzu (c. 500 BC)

Why succumb? Why not succeed as a manager – develop effective, relevant communication skills!

Reference

Kolb, D. A., Rubin, I. M., and McIntyre, J. A. (1971), *Organisational Behaviour*, Prentice Hall, Englewood Cliffs, NJ.

Index